PRAISE FOR NEVER FORGET

"I devoured it in one sitting. Such a wonderfully written collection of people's experiences - it really got under the skin of each of them."

TONY WRIGHT - FILM-MAKER AND PRODUCER

"The stories in Jo's book (and the lives of her subjects) have amazing plots, dramatic changes of fortune, crisis, conflict and resolution, accompanied by persistent threat - all the elements of great fiction. We meet sharply drawn characters, people like us, doing what they can to survive, with great modesty and great courage. Yet this isn't fiction. These are real stories, lives documented of people we might have known, who lived down the street or around the corner, and knew our parents or grandparents."

IAN LATHAM - FOUNDER OF NZDIVCAV.ORG

NEVER FORGET

SIX EXTRAORDINARY WORLD WAR II STORIES
OF COURAGE, SURVIVAL AND HOPE

JO BAILEY

AUDREY
PUBLISHING

CREDITS

Copyright: Audrey Publishing

Second edition paperback 2022

ISBN 978-0-473-47556-7

Written by: Jo Bailey

Cover design: Craig Morgan

Cover image: Cropped image 'Polish refugee children arriving in Wellington on board the ship General Randall'. Pascoe, John Dobree,

1908-1972 Photographic albums, prints and negatives. Ref: 1/2-003629-F. Alexander Turnbull Library, Wellington, New Zealand.

By the same author:

From Rag Trade to Mag Trade: The Annah Stretton Business Story
The Long Way Home (Available on Amazon)
When the Doors Go Up

Visit www.jobailey.com for more information and to sign up for Jo's newsletter. Find Jo Bailey Author on Facebook and Instagram.

ABOUT JO BAILEY

Throughout more than 30 years working in print media in New Zealand, Jo Bailey has written thousands of news, feature and promotional stories, which have appeared in a variety of national and niche publications. Her features on high profile people have included everyone from rock stars and politicians to top sportspeople and television personalities. Since 2000, Jo has run her own writing, editing and publishing business, supporting clients across a range of media. In 2001, she was the co-writer of a musical black comedy, *Robin Hood, a Twisted Sherwood Tale.* Jo is also a writing coach, and through her Writing Life Stories Your Way workshops, helps people to tell their own or family stories.

Never Forget is Jo's fourth non-fiction book.

Jo lives in Christchurch, New Zealand. She is the proud mother of two gorgeous grown-ups, and Jasper, the much-adored cat.

www.jobailey.com

For Hannah and Riley, my light, my loves

CONTENTS

INTRODUCTION

"These boys gave their lives and some came home badly injured, and for some families, life would never be the same. We should always remember, we should never forget, and we should teach the children to remember."
Dame Vera Lynn

At the United Kingdom's VE Day Diamond Jubilee Concert at Trafalgar Square, London in 2005, the 'Forces' Sweetheart', Dame Vera Lynn, made a surprise appearance, singing her wartime anthem *We'll Meet Again*. She also delivered the important message that we should 'never forget' the sacrifice made by those who so bravely fought to preserve democracy and liberty during World War II.

In these uncertain times, when the divisions between nations seem wider than ever, the importance of remembering and honouring stories which show the impact of war has perhaps never been greater.

The stories in this book feature New Zealanders, however only the two servicemen, Naylor Hillary and Harry Spencer were born in this country.

The rest are stories about children-of-war from the Netherlands,

Poland, the Dutch East Indies (Indonesia) and the United Kingdom, who one way or another, after their traumatic wartime experiences, managed to find a safe haven in New Zealand, a tiny country at the bottom of the world.

Although the brave servicemen, evacuees and migrants who feature in *Never Forget* forged happy lives post World War II, they always carried their wartime memories with them, the horrors they witnessed, and their personal battles for survival and freedom.

Later in their lives, they chose to tell their extraordinary stories, which are testament to the power and resilience of the human spirit.

These stories remind us of the futility of war, its impact on all citizens, and the lessons we can learn from the past.

Today, the world faces extraordinary challenges. If we can work together and focus on the things that bind us as human beings, rather than descending into battle over the things that divide us, perhaps we truly can make a difference for future generations.

———

1

BRAM

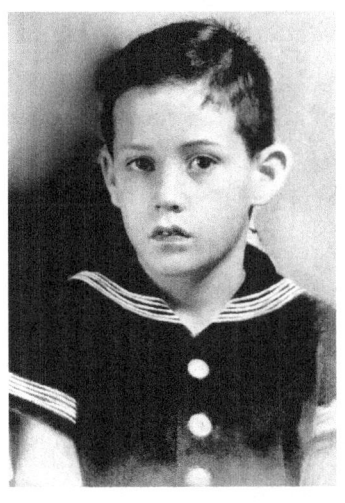

THE SIGHT of three Australian soldiers emerging from the jungle in West Java in 1942, would never leave Bram Uljee's mind.

"I was just seven years old when these bronzed, tall Australians wearing slouch hats and carrying rifles, burst out of the jungle. They made a huge impression on me."

The soldiers had escaped from Singapore and were making their way through Japanese-occupied Indonesia (then the Dutch East Indies).

Their journey had taken them through the isolated mountain ranges where Bram's father (also named Bram), a Dutch tea planter, was in charge of the large Sambawa tea plantation and its 2000 Indonesian workers.

"I remember the soldiers staying for lunch and having quite long discussions with my mother and father, who both spoke very good English. Once they left, my parents told me the men had escaped from Singapore, and after working their way down the coast in canoes, had travelled overland, with the intention of reaching the south coast of West Java, not far from us, to see if they could get a fishing boat to Darwin.

"The soldiers tried to persuade my parents to take us with them, as the situation under Japanese occupation was becoming more perilous. However my father felt it was too risky to attempt the trip in an open boat with two young children."

The Japanese Empire's conquest and occupation of the Dutch East Indies, from March 1942 until the end of World War II, effectively ended 300 years of Dutch colonial presence. It proved to be one of the most critical periods in Indonesian history, and drastically changed the lives of the Uljee family forever.

Bram was born in Indonesia, but was fifth-generation Dutch. Until the war his family had led a relatively sheltered and privileged life at Sambawa, which was on the upper slopes of the active volcanic Mount Galunggung.

"Although we were very isolated and living high up just below the frost line, we were part of a colonial culture where money was virtually no object. My mother had a chauffeur, maids, a cook, and gardeners, and I was taught by a governess in the tennis club pavilion with the other children on the estate. I also had an Indonesian nanny, who was almost like a second mother, and who taught me values which are still with me today."

There was always lots of social activity at the tea estate, with lavish dinner parties, ladies' afternoon teas and bridge games until late into the night.

"It was a marvellous childhood. We lived right on the edge of the jungle, where there were monkeys and other exotic animals. I had an aviary with many different types of birds which an Indonesian boy looked after for me."

Bram used to get into mischief during his parents' regular afternoon siesta and to curb his naughtiness was banned from leaving the house until the quiet time was over.

"I used to get bored and wasn't much of a reader, so I would open the glass front on my parents' beautiful Swiss clock, and move the hands to 3pm, which was the time I was allowed out of the house. Unfortunately I didn't get away with this for too long."

Bram said his father was a fair man who was well respected by his workers.

"He became responsible for their health and wellbeing, and the workers even looked to the 'big white boss' to settle their disputes."

The Sambawa tea estate in West Java

Natural elements made life precarious in the region, which was prone to numerous large earthquakes and flooding when heavy rain fell further up the mountain slopes. Bridges were regularly washed away, which could leave the estate cut off for weeks at a time. During those periods, Bram's family had to rely on a cableway for supplies. One benefit of the tea estate's isolation meant in the early part of

World War II, and in the months after the Dutch capitulated to the Japanese in 1942, life there simply carried on.

"We were able to bide our time in the beginning. The reality of war wasn't really brought home until we were made to fly a large white surrender flag from the main building on the tea estate, and I saw a Japanese war plane circling overhead to check us out."

Bram said after the unexpected arrival of the Australian soldiers, his father became aware of the growing danger for his family, and heard that Dutch people were being rounded up by the Japanese.

Bram Uljee Senior at the family's townhouse in Bandung at the outbreak of war

"My father was in the Royal Netherlands East Indies Army and knew he would eventually be called back to barracks and interned. Before that happened he planned an escape route so the rest of us could get to my mother's parents' small dairy farm at Bandung, quite some distance away, where our family also had a town house. My mother's family had some German heritage so he thought we would be safer there."

Petrol was impounded so it wasn't possible for the family to travel by car. Instead, Bram's father bought a buggy and 16 horses, which he stationed along a route to a rail-head. Once the family reached the railhead, they would be able to catch a train to a station near Bram's grandparents' farm.

"Soon after, my father had to report to barracks and was promptly imprisoned. Life carried on without him for the next couple of months until one day we heard through the bush telegraph the Japanese were rounding up all Europeans, men women and children, whether they were in the army or not. My mother knew it was too dangerous to stay, so the time had come to make our escape."

After packing the few possessions they could carry, Bram, his mother Ellen, and his brother Don (who was five years younger), loaded up the buggy and at five o'clock one morning left their old life behind forever. Bram sat next to the driver, with the beautiful wooden clock he used to tamper with during his parents' afternoon rest, lying between his feet. It was one of the few special possessions they managed to take with them. It took all day to travel to the nearest railhead by buggy, with many horse changes along the way. On their arrival at dusk, they were met by a friend who had agreed to put them up for the night. The following morning, heavily disguised, they boarded a train for the half-day journey to the station nearest Bram's grandparents' farm.

"A Japanese soldier sat opposite us in the train carriage for part of the journey. He was the first Japanese person we had laid eyes on. He seemed reasonably relaxed but my mother was frightened and so were my brother and I. It was a tense journey."

They finally made it to safety at the farm near Bandung, a city, which prior to the war had been a resort for tea plantation owners, with luxury hotels, cafes, and boutiques.

"We were lucky because my mother's family had the surname Ritter, and my uncle, who was single and six feet tall, looked very German. When the Japanese came to check us out, my uncle told them he was German and that my mother, brother and I were his wife and kids."

Bram said the Japanese lost interest in them after that, apart from requisitioning the milk produced by the 150 cows on the farm.

"My uncle was told he had to supply the Japanese, rather than take the milk to market. He had to wear a special badge on his shoulder, which led him into all sorts of places other people couldn't go."

The farm was a safe haven for Bram's family, who sheltered there for most of the war. His mother, Ellen managed to get hold of a clandestine radio, which she would listen to before dawn, in a room blackened by heavy curtains.

"My mother would get the news from the BBC, which would be passed down a chain of people in different areas. She was very brave."

Bram (right), his mother Ellen, and brother, Don in a portrait painted by a Chinese artist. Cameras were banned by the Japanese during the war.

Not long after their arrival, the family was given the heart-wrenching news that Bram's father had been interned in a prisoner-of-war barracks in a neighbouring town.

"We were determined to see him. However it was too dangerous to travel by open road, so we had to take shortcuts instead. We would leave early in the morning and ride our bikes along very narrow paths beside the paddy fields."

The Japanese had enclosed the barracks inside tall bamboo matted fences with barbed wire around the top.

"We managed to find out which part of the camp my father was in. If he and the other prisoners stood on the windowsills inside the barracks, they could just see us over the bamboo structures. We were able to have a bit of a conversation, and throw them medicine or messages wrapped around stones."

It wasn't long before the Japanese became aware of what was happening and raised the fences even higher.

By this time it had become more dangerous for women to move around.

This restricted the family's ability to visit Bram's father at the camp, so they attempted to meet the prisoners when they were out on work parties instead.

"It was my job to station myself behind trees or on an empty section to see which way the work parties went after they came out of the main gates at the barracks. I would tell Mum and she and a group of women would follow the work parties and almost harass the Japanese guards to let them see their husbands."

Finally it became too dangerous for the women to visit at all and it was left to the children to try and smuggle in messages or medicine to the prisoners.

By this time Bram was just eight years old. He remembered feeling defiant rather than scared about the family's predicament, although frightening experiences were never far away.

"One day I was being chased by some Japanese soldiers, when an Indonesian woman came to my rescue. She grabbed me, took me into her house and changed me out of my clothes into a dress and bonnet. I rushed out the back door, grabbed a bike and rode off dressed as a girl."

On another occasion a local boy told Bram the work party was having a break in an empty building nearby and the sentry might let him in to speak with his father.

"I found the building and the sentry said I could go in. The prisoners were sitting in very cramped conditions with their knees right up to their chins. I had to almost goose step over them to get to my father, who was recovering from a bad bout of pneumonia. He was so happy to see me. We embraced and had a good talk. It was a privileged and proud moment for me."

Bram said he always felt grateful to the sentry on duty that day.

"I wish I could have thanked him for what he did. I think he was Korean, one of many who would have been compulsorily drafted into the Japanese army. He was a lovely guy, a shining apple in a box of rotten ones."

In 1944, the family learned Bram's father, uncle and cousin were being taken by rail to Jakarta where they were to board a small cargo ship, a steamer called *Junyō Maru*. It was one of the many 'hell ships' used for transporting Allied prisoners during the Pacific War. The ship's destination was Padang on the south coast of Sumatra, where Bram's father and the other prisoners were to be put to work on the infamous Pekanbaru

Railway, which later became known as the Pekanbaru Death Railway.

Conditions on the *Junyō Maru* were appalling. Around 2300 Dutch, British, Australian, Indonesian and a few American prisoners-of-war were crowded on board alongside 4200 Javanese slave labourers. The ship had been fitted with extra decks constructed of bamboo scaffolding where its human cargo was forced to sit, stand, or if they were lucky, lie down. Some were permanently housed on the ship's upper deck, where they were exposed to brutal tropical heat during the day, and windy, cold temperatures at night. Many of the prisoners were already sick and emaciated. There was not enough water, and the only toilets were a few boxes suspended outboard on the upper deck.

"The prisoners were crammed in like battery hens in a cage. Once they sat down they couldn't move. My father told me many of the men were ill with dysentery but they couldn't get to a toilet, so human excrement accumulated in the holds."

The stench of human beings and their waste was overbearing. Many of the sick and weak on board died, or came close to death as the journey progressed. On 18 September 1944, when the *Junyō Maru* was close to its destination, it was torpedoed by the British submarine HMS *Tradewind*, which had been cruising in the patrol area. The *Tradewind* had already successfully targeted other Japanese cargo ships in the vicinity, but by the time its crew spotted the *Junyō Maru*, they were having trouble with the submarine's radar and high-power periscope.

The Lieutenant Commander had to rely on a low-power periscope instead, which was inaccurate over a long distance.

He could see the *Junyō Maru* was close to fully loaded, but without his high-power periscope, couldn't guess what the load was.

"The Japanese were not flying the prisoner-of-war flag, so he had no idea the vessel was a prisoner-of-war transporter. He decided to sink it."

The *Junyō Maru*.

When the torpedoes hit, pandemonium and panic broke out immediately. Many of the prisoners on board were killed instantly, and others in the less damaged part of the ship desperately tried to escape. There was only one staircase in the hold where Bram's father was being held, which was quickly overrun with men trying to get out. Bram's father was thrust upwards in the throng, and when he got on to the deck, the water was already level with it.

Fortunately sea conditions were calm but the water was already thick with bodies. Life boats were launched and filled with Japanese soldiers. Any prisoners trying to hang on to the side were swiftly dealt with.

"My father told me some horrific stories of prisoners having their hands chopped off or their skulls opened with swords."

Many of the prisoners clung to the *Junyō Maru* until it eventually sank. As night fell, frightened survivors held on to makeshift rafts and debris, crying out for help.

At dawn, a Japanese destroyer which had been searching for the British submarine, returned to pick up the Japanese survivors from the lifeboats. Some of surviving prisoners were also pulled onto the ship. They had already been in the water for some time.

Bram's cousin drowned in the disaster, but his father and uncle were able to swim out to the destroyer and hoist themselves up onto the low deck by climbing ropes hanging over the side. Once on board, they and the other exhausted survivors, were forced to stand to attention. They weren't allowed to sit or rest.

"The Japanese only wanted to rescue those men considered fit enough to work. Anyone too weak to stand was simply thrown back into the water and had to swim for it."

Around 5620 prisoners-of-war and Javanese slave labourers died in the sinking of the *Junyō Maru*, making it one of the largest maritime disasters of World War II.

Just 880 of the prisoners on board eventually made it to shore and were immediately drafted into groups to work on the Pekanbaru Railway.

Ironically, it was the Dutch who had originally investigated the possibility of building a railway line to connect the east and west coasts of Sumatra, in a bid to access coal fields in the interior of the country.

They scrapped the plans when they realised the impossibly rugged jungle that would have to be cut through, and how difficult it would be to build rail bridges during monsoon season. Then there were the risks of malaria and dangerous animals such as tigers and bears to the workers.

After the Imperial Japanese Army invaded in 1942, they decided to put the plans into action. Constructing a 220km railway line, which dissected the country and connected the river port of Pekanbaru to the town of Muaro, would enable them to move troops and coal from coast to coast without encountering Allied warships at sea.

The Japanese forced around 120,000 Indonesian labourers to work on the railway, with only around 16,000 surviving the backbreaking work, appalling conditions, and constant physical and mental abuse from their Japanese overseers.

Prisoners-of-war on the Pekanbaru Death Railway
*Photograph sourced from the Argus Collection and
supplied by Jeffery Farrell.*

Later around 5000 Allied prisoners-of-war (mainly Dutch, but also some British, American and New Zealand troops) were brought in to supplement the dwindling workforce.

They were placed into 18 camps along the length of the railway. Most of the men who survived the sinking of the *Junyō Maru* were said to have ended up in Camps 3 and 4, where they were tasked with building a rail bridge.

Things went from bad to worse for Bram's father, who after surviving the terrible sinking of the *Junyō Maru*, was forced to endure atrocious conditions and horrific treatment at the hands of the Japanese and their Korean prison guards in the camp, said Bram.

"Dad said the Korean guards were also turned into sadists under Japanese indoctrination."

The prisoners were regularly beaten, worked from daylight until dark, and given only meagre rations. There was no defence against the hordes of mosquitoes, and the men had little or no possessions, with only a Japanese loin cloth to wear.

Bram's father told him the prisoners slept on wooden struts in huge sheds. When it flooded during the rainy season the Japanese guards would paddle through in canoes to check on them. The prisoners got all sorts of diseases, including malaria, pneumonia and beriberi. There were no anaesthetics and doctors operated using scalpels made from bamboo.

"To keep the sick going, they fed them maggots for protein. They also used maggots to eat the dead flesh around their wounds."

The big cats in the jungle were a constant source of danger for the prisoners, said Bram.

"Dad told me a two-metre long tiger would pick a man off the line like a cat would take a mouse. Prisoners were made to light fires at night outside the Japanese guards' quarters to keep the tigers away."

With only meagre rations, the prisoners were starving and would eat whatever they could find in the jungle. On one occasion they made a meal out of a large python snake, which had a huge bulge. After killing it, the men found it had just swallowed a wild pig. The prisoners were so hungry they ate them both.

Bram kept the original postcards sent by his father from the prisoner-of-war camp, which were delivered through the Red Cross.

"My father was only allowed to write 30 or 40 heavily censored words about once a year. It wasn't much, but at least we knew he was still alive. In one postcard, through overt language, he was able to let us know my cousin had drowned in the torpedoing. When he later wrote that the Japanese were treating him well, we knew it was far from the truth."

———

Back at the farm, there was no schooling for Bram and his brother, as the Japanese forbade it. However Bram and his brother were secretly home-schooled by their teacher mother.

With no books or writing paper to use, they had to write on a slate with a long, thin piece of chalk, called a griffel in Dutch. Once the slate was full, it was wiped clean with a wet cloth before the boys could start writing again, making it a very slow process for them to learn.

"I don't know how Mum was able to teach us and keep us alive. We suffered lots of tropical ulcers, and medicines were hard to come by. We had half a bottle of petrol, which she used to treat the worst of our ulcers."

The only way to access medicine was through an extremely dangerous chain, that Bram wouldn't gain a true insight into until he was much older.

"I was shocked to discover that some Dutch women had bravely prostituted themselves to the Japanese in order to obtain medicine which they would pass on to the sick and dying."

Bram was sometimes sent out on his bike after curfew to collect the medicine.

"I was told where to go and who I had to meet. It was terribly dark as the lights were dimmed for fear of an Allied attack. In Indonesia most of the highways and streets were lined with big trees. As long as I could see the stars in the sky, I knew I was riding in the middle of the road. It was an important job so I had to push my fears aside."

One night, as Bram was riding uphill, he collided with someone coming the other way.

"The chap was out doing the same thing as me and we had an almighty crash in the pitch black. As we tried to untangle our bikes we heard shooting nearby so we jumped into a drain and waited until it stopped. We talked quietly to each other but I never saw his face. Then we said our goodbyes and carried on."

A number of Dutch women were also captured and forced into sex slavery in the 'comfort stations' at Japanese army camps where they endured systematic beatings and were raped day and night by the soldiers. Bram still has vivid memories of the Korean comfort women used by the Japanese soldiers at Bandung, but at the time he didn't understand what was happening to them.

"I found out later the military were given tear-off cards with a perforation in the middle, red for soldiers, and blue for officers. When they visited the women they would give them half the card, which the women could exchange for food. If they didn't amass tokens they didn't eat. A lot of the women got venereal disease and were simply discarded. It was terrible."

The treatment of women by the Japanese military wasn't fully revealed until decades after the war. Many of the earliest comfort women were Japanese prostitutes. When greater numbers of women were required, the military coerced more women from Japan and its colonies, particularly Korea, telling them they were needed as factory workers or nurses. These women were unwittingly forced into sexual slavery instead. Many thousands of other women were kidnapped and subjected to the same fate at Japanese Army camps, where they endured horrific abuse. Some were raped 30 to 40 times a day. It is believed around three quarters of the comfort women may have died during the war, with many survivors left infertile due to sexual trauma and sexually transmitted diseases.

———

Bram's family's dairy farm at Bandung was near a military aerodrome. One morning they were surprised to see Japanese soldiers driving trucks into their fodder paddock.

Soon after, searchlights and field guns were set up, not far from the family's homestead.

"Kids being kids, we couldn't keep away and the Japanese were actually quite friendly. They allowed us to turn the large wheels that raised and lowered the gun and search light. As they had not seen blonde children before, my brother was quite a novelty to them, but when Mum found out, we were well and truly banned from going anywhere near them."

Bram's mother continued to listen to her secret radio, and from a BBC report in early August 1945 she heard that atom bombs had been dropped on Hiroshima and Nagasaki killing at least 129,000 people. The Japanese surrendered a few days later.

"The sight of the American planes parachuting food to us is still firmly fixed in my mind. The supplies were expressly made for undernourished people and manufactured to make it hard for people to gorge themselves. Some who did, got very sick."

Bram said during those dark days the words of his wise old Christian grandma gave him great strength.

"She said 'whenever you face danger, say that you are a child of God'. This was deeply entrenched in my mind and I believe saved me from great danger more than once."

Although liberation from the Japanese was imminent, the Uljees continued to wait for news of Bram's father. Construction of the Pekanbaru line was completed on 15 August 1945, the same day Japan capitulated.

It was never used for its intended purpose, to carry coal from the mines in West Sumatra to Pekanbaru.

Instead the railway was used to transport freed prisoners-of-war. Not long after, it was abandoned and reclaimed by the jungle. All those poor souls who had endured such treacherous conditions and ill treatment, or who lost their lives while working on the railway, had done so in vain.

Before the atom bombs were dropped, Bram's father, uncle, and three cousins, who were also prisoners, had faced near certain death in the prisoner-of-war camps.

The Japanese War Ministry had sent out a directive ordering the execution of all Allied prisoners should Japan be invaded. Bram's father and the other prisoners had heard rumours they were at risk of being slaughtered, so the sudden end to the war was a great relief.

Immediately after the Japanese surrender, their captors in the prison camps fled, and Allied planes were soon flying overhead dropping food, clothing and medical supplies.

Prisoners in their barracks on the Pekanbaru Death Railway.
Photograph sourced from the Argus Collection and supplied by
Jeffery Farrell.

Bram's family rejoiced and looked forward to the return of their loved ones but it was another six months before Bram's father and uncle were finally reunited with their families.

They were among less than 100 men left of the 880 sent to Pekanbaru after the torpedoing of the Junyō Maru.

The men had survived near starvation, brutality and disease and were weak with malnutrition.

"Lady Mountbatten cried at the sight of the prisoners when she visited them shortly after their liberation as they had been reduced to skin and bone. Dad was about 90kg when he went in and only 40kg when he came out."

Most of the tens of thousands of men who lost their lives during the construction of the Pekanbaru Railway, still lay buried in forgotten graves in the thick jungle, alongside the remnants of the abandoned tracks.

Liberated prisoners in Sumatra. *Photograph from the Argos Collection courtesy of Jeffery Farrell.*

Bram's family couldn't believe it when five out of their six family members who were captured and imprisoned by the Japanese, made it back alive.

"My three surviving cousins also had a terrible time. One was sent to work on the Burma Railway and the other two had to work in coal mines in Japan. As one of my cousins was being evacuated by the Americans from a prisoner-of-war camp towards the Port of Yokahama and then to the Philippines, he recalled seeing city after city in Japan which had been razed by American bombers. He said you could read a book at night by the light of the fires. There is no doubt the Japanese people also suffered greatly."

Unfortunately the family's joy at the end of the war proved short-lived, as in the six months before their men returned to the family, Bram's mother was forced to keep her children safe in the face of yet more extreme danger. The Uljee family owned a townhouse at

Bandung, and after the liberation, Ellen Uljee confronted the Japanese officer who had been living there during the war, telling him to leave.

"He wasn't having a bar of it but after they argued, he agreed we could move into the pavilion next to the main house, which was similar to a self-contained unit. It was a very strange situation," said Bram.

The family hoped for peace and a gradual return to normality but more trouble was brewing. The destruction of the Dutch colonial regime and the facilitation of Indonesian nationalism under the Japanese occupation had created the conditions for a bid for Indonesian independence. Allied troops had largely by-passed Indonesia so it was still under Japanese occupation at the time of their surrender.

"Everything was chaotic. We had fallen from World War II into the Indonesian Freedom War and were totally defenceless. It was a very bad and scary time."

Some of the heaviest battles during the independence struggles happened in and around Bandung. The bitter uprising became increasingly violent with Dutch residents a prime target.

"We had to be vigilant and make sure all the windows and doors were locked at night. Mum used to place tin cans on the inside of the door handles to wake us if there were intruders, as the cans landing on the tile floor would make quite a racket."

One day Bram's mother heard a large, murderous group approaching their street from across a huge field.

"She dragged my brother out of the bathroom and the three of us fled on our bikes. An armed guard at a crossroads was cutting everybody off but just as we approached he turned his back to look at a pretty Indonesian woman. We managed to race past him and even now I can feel the hairs on the back of my neck tickle as we waited for a bullet to strike – but thankfully it never came."

The family's townhouse and many other homes were burned to the ground that day with around 60 Dutch people murdered. The British and Ghurkha troops had only just landed and didn't have sufficient numbers to protect them. With Dutch homes burning, the British started to engage with the Indonesians but realised they needed backup, so commandeered some Japanese tanks to help them fight.

"We watched the battle from my aunty's terrace. It was amazing to see British and Ghurkha troops on Japanese Bren gun carriers going into battle. How quickly our allegiance changed when our lives were in danger – we cheered them all."

Bram said the Ghurkhas were among the best soldiers of the British Army and he recalled seeing wounded men walking back from the fighting.

"The battle got more intense and bullets started to fly around. It was too much for Mum and we were ordered to the back of the house. Towards dusk Mum led us away from the fighting towards a safe area, where that night, we slept on the ground."

Having lost their home, and most of their few possessions, they returned to live with Bram's aunty. Around this time Bram got into mischief with some of his friends, when they stole a small Japanese utility truck.

"My friend had no driving experience but somehow he managed. We piled on the back and off we went for a joy ride. As we came past our house, I waved to my elderly Grandma and she spotted me and told Mum. We had a great ride in the hills until we ran out of petrol, and simply pushed the ute down into a ravine. In those days anything Japanese was fair game."

In the early stages of the Indonesian Freedom War, the British took a military hold on Java's major cities and gave Indonesian combatants in Bandung an ultimatum to leave the city. As they left in March 1946, the combatants deliberately set much of the southern part of the city alight, in an event known as the 'Bandung Sea of Fire'. Despite the danger, Bram's family managed to stay safe until his father was liberated from the prisoner-of-war camp. His parents were keen to make a fresh start away from the conflict and by chance a few months later, they heard about an agreement between the Dutch and

New Zealand governments to evacuate two boatloads of Dutch people from Indonesia to New Zealand, where they would be given respite from the conflict.

"We were lucky to be selected and shortly after found ourselves on the SS *Tasman* bound for New Zealand. Conditions on board were very basic. My dad and I were quartered in the forward hold, sleeping on army stretchers in long rows. The din of the clattering stretchers when the bow of the ship rose and fell on the waves made sleeping difficult. I soon discovered it was much better to sleep under a structure out on the deck."

There was an unwelcome surprise for the family when they arrived at Brisbane and learned the Australian Waterside Union had declared all Dutch ships 'black' in sympathy with the Indonesian Freedom Movement. This included the SS *Tasman*, so there were no tugs to assist it to berth. Bram said nobody was allowed off the ship and no supplies were allowed on board, however, help was soon at hand from the 'black ban breakers'.

"We were amazed when a truck pulled up with warm clothing for us to go into a New Zealand winter, donated by David Jones, a big department store in Brisbane."

Bram said he found the watersiders' rationale despicable, declaring a ship black when it was carrying evacuees from a war-torn country.

"The Australian watersiders were extremely militant and even tried to sabotage the American war effort."

Eventually the ship got away when the Captain quietly slipped the mooring lines one night at high tide. With dimmed lights it floated down the Brisbane River, the engines were started and it headed for New Zealand.

A tumultuous welcome greeted the SS *Tasman* when it docked in Auckland, New Zealand on Good Friday, 1946. Bram said members of the Auckland Travel Club lined up in their cars to greet the ship. After they were welcomed, the evacuees were driven to a vacant American Services Hospital on Market Road in Remuera. Dubbed

'Camp Oranje', it was run by the Netherlands East Indies Welfare Organisation. The Uljee's driver was a lady named Florence Grant, who ended up becoming a good family friend.

"Florence took great care of our family and was instrumental in getting us settled in New Zealand. Many doors were opened for us through her brother-in-law, Eddy Gordon, who was a Member of Parliament for Rangitikei. I later worked on the Gordon farm near Marton and always maintained strong links with the family."

The Uljees were fortunate to make it to New Zealand at all, as around the time of their arrival, the Consul-General for the Netherlands in New Zealand, Jonkheer van Panhuys said a shortage of foreign currency had caused a considerable reduction in the Dutch evacuation scheme, with only a few hundred evacuees able to come to New Zealand instead of the original 3000 which had been planned for.

A report in the New Zealand Herald on Easter Saturday 1946 said:

The second and final draft of Dutch evacuees to reach New Zealand from the Netherlands East Indies arrived at Auckland yesterday morning in the passenger ship 'Tasman', after a voyage of 22 days from Batavia, via Brisbane. Consisting of 433 Dutch nationals, 261 of whom are to stay in Auckland, the party was more than favourably impressed with the reception they received. Presenting a slightly different picture from their countrymen who arrived in New Zealand in February, the Dutch looked much healthier, due to the greater time they had had to recuperate, and were better equipped with clothes, although these were mainly of army issue. After the years they had spent in Japanese prison camps they were eagerly looking forward to a few months in New Zealand. Eighty-six of those who are to stay in Auckland are children under 12.

In the article, Mr van Panhuys said it was 'great pity' it would be the last draft of evacuees coming to New Zealand, as the scheme had been a success. He expected all evacuees to have left New Zealand again within six months. However many of these first groups of arrivals were eventually able to become New Zealand residents and impressed local employers so much, they set the scene for mass immigration by the Dutch into New Zealand in the 1950s. An intake of 10,583 Dutch settlers was later recorded between July 1951 and June 1954.

The Uljee family was well looked after at 'Camp Oranje', where they ate plenty of ice cream, drank gallons of milk, and their health improved dramatically.

They later rented a house at 29 Liverpool Street in Royal Oak, with three other evacuated families. It was here that another near tragedy was averted.

The women were unfamiliar with cooking on a coal gas stove and accidentally left it on before they went to bed. As gas flowed through the house, Bram, who was sleeping in an upstairs room, woke and realised something was wrong.

"I had to fight to wake up properly, but managed to get up and wake Dad. At 4am we all ended up on the lawn outside, with the windows open, airing the house."

As some of the earliest Dutch immigrants to New Zealand, Bram and his family had to make some significant adjustments. Being thrust into a free country also heightened the magnitude of the family's war experiences, which started to become a burden for Bram.

"I became aware I was different to my school mates but with no counselling available, my family and I just had to get on with it and try to mentally heal ourselves. Thankfully it is very different today."

The family also discovered they would be monitored wherever they went. Their temporary identification papers had to be stamped at a police station every time they visited a new city or region. Later, when it came time to apply for their new New Zealand passports, the Uljees had to gloss over their ethnicity. Bram said back then, Australia and New Zealand had a covert 'all white' immigration policy, with dark skinned people not allowed entry. Although of Dutch descent, Bram had some Indonesian blood, and was olive-skinned like his mother, although his father and brother were both fair haired with blue eyes.

The Uljee family in New Zealand in 1947.

The photographer who took the family's photographs for their new passports knew about the discrimination and to help them, brought in some extra screens to reflect the light and make Bram and his mother appear whiter.

With almost no money, it wasn't easy for the family to fit into life in this new country.

"We were gaunt and looked upon as gypsies by some New Zealanders who had never seen foreigners before. There were still a lot of wonderful people who welcomed us though, such as the returned servicemen who understood what we had been through. I recall them giving us money to buy ice creams."

The family was in New Zealand for several months before, under the terms of their evacuee status, they were required to return to the

Dutch East Indies, where on 24 October 1946, Ellen gave birth to the family's youngest child, a daughter, also named Ellen. While in the Dutch East Indies, the family applied to become permanent residents of New Zealand.

"A few months later, we all came back to New Zealand, with the plan for me to be left at boarding school here, while the rest of my family went back to Bandung to sell our remaining possessions in anticipation of us leaving for good. However, once we returned to New Zealand, my uncle said things back at Bandung had become too dangerous again because of the Freedom War, so my parents decided we should all stay in New Zealand. We started our new life here with just the five suitcases we arrived with. I don't know how my parents managed," said Bram.

Bram's father was by now in his forties and after all the trauma he had experienced in the prisoner-of-war camps, found it a challenge to adjust to his new life. He was keen to find peace and make the best of the situation, but found it difficult to get a good job, said Bram.

"At the time New Zealanders were generally unwilling to employ foreigners as there was a bit of stigma attached to it. Having lost all our possessions in the wars we needed money desperately but my father's overseas qualifications weren't recognised here. This was difficult for him, as he was a proud, capable man who had led 2000 workers before being taken prisoner."

Bram's father initially had to carve out a living doing hard manual work at the gigantic freezing works at Westfield, which was one of the only places migrants could make good money.

He later worked as a research officer with the Department of Scientific and Industrial Research (DSIR).

"The tough physical work at the freezing works was really hard for my father after what he had endured at the camps."

Bram's mother Ellen also had to leave her privileged past well and truly behind.

"My parents eventually managed to buy a big house, and after doing some alterations, took in several boarders to help pay the mortgage. My father used to go to the Auckland wharf when migrant ships came in, and would talk to the new arrivals, offering them board and giving them advice on how to get a job."

Without a car, it was a challenge for Bram's mother to gather the supplies needed to feed these extra mouths. She used to take a big trundler to the shops and pull it back behind her, laden with supplies, groceries and meat.

This was quite an adjustment after having a cook and a chauffeur who had driven her everywhere, back in the Dutch East Indies.

Like his father, most of the migrants ended up working at the freezing works, with a few later bringing girlfriends out to New Zealand and getting married there, said Bram.

"Most started off in a very modest way. A lot of New Zealanders wouldn't live in the hovels some of the migrants started their married life in. It is amazing how well many of them did in later life."

Despite the setbacks, the Uljee family slowly climbed the ladder to a good life in New Zealand. Bram attended Market Road Primary School in Remuera and later Auckland Grammar School before studying at Massey University.

Like his father, Bram worked at the freezing works during school and university holidays, doing long hours for good money. He also worked on a number of farms.

Incredibly, at Christmas 1953, he cheated death once again.

"I was working on the Gordon family's sheep farm near Marton and was booked on the night express to travel home to Auckland for Christmas. My boss, Graeme Gordon, decided since everything was up-to-date on the farm, I could go home a day early, so he rebooked my ticket. I was safely home with my parents on Christmas Eve when I learned the train I should have been on had plunged into the flooded Whangaehu River at Tangawai."

The disaster was caused by the collapse of the tephra dam holding back nearby Mount Ruapehu's crater lake, which created a large lahar in the Whangaehu River. This destroyed one of the bridge piers at Tangawai, just minutes before the train reached the bridge.

Known as the 'Tangawai Disaster' this is still New Zealand's worst rail accident, with 151 of the 285 passengers and crew on board perishing. Many of them had been heading home for Christmas armed with presents for their families and friends.

Unfortunately for the Uljee family, the disaster also scuppered their opportunity to meet Queen Elizabeth II and the Duke of Edinburgh from the United Kingdom, who were visiting New Zealand at the time. One of the royal couple's engagements in Auckland was to attend festivities at the Western Springs Stadium, which included a fireworks display.

"My parents' house overlooked the open stadium and as the weather forecast was not promising, Auckland City Council asked if it would be possible for the Queen and Duke to watch the fireworks from our large covered verandah, with the accompanying dignitaries seated in our terraced garden below. There was a flurry of activity as council workers gave our garden a huge makeover, and my father busily painted the very long, wide porch around the house."

On 23rd of December, when all was in order for the festivities, there was a rehearsal and a policeman was stationed in front of the house. Unfortunately, the following day, the Tangiwai Disaster occurred and all royal engagements were cancelled. Bram says the Uljee family would have been thrilled to host the Queen and Duke but it was not to be.

A few years later, the impact of the trauma Bram's father had suffered would prove too much. Just as the family had saved enough for a better home, better car, and a boat to go fishing, he died of a heart attack when Bram was aged in his thirties.

"My father went all too soon, like many others who had lived through such terrible ordeals during the war."

Bram had deep respect for both his parents and for the courage and resilience they showed throughout their lives.

After his father passed away, Bram's mother kept the boarding house going and then converted the house into two flats, which continued to provide her with an income.

She later moved to a Dutch village in Henderson in Auckland where she lived until she was 87 years old.

"My mother was a great lady, whose bravery was instrumental in keeping my brother and I alive during the war, and who worked so hard alongside my father to rebuild our lives in New Zealand. I feel blessed to be living in this privileged and free country. Every time I come back from overseas I say, thank goodness I'm home."

New Zealand may have been a very different place had the Allied forces not defeated the Japanese in the Battle of the Coral Sea (the first air-sea battle in history, in May 1942) and the Battle of Midway the following month, which further turned the tide in the Allies favour.

The Japanese were seeking to control the Coral Sea with an invasion of Port Moresby in southeast New Guinea but their plans were intercepted by Allied code breakers.

Historians tend to believe the threat of a Japanese invasion to New Zealand was slight, however, there

Bram Uljee Senior in 1965, not long before he died of a heart attack

was genuine fear among the population, particularly in exposed coastal areas during the early part of the war before the two big air-sea battles were won by the Allied forces.

Every city in New Zealand had trench digging, air raid practices and emergency planning.

"After the war, a friend of my mother was told by a Japanese officer the Japanese had planned to invade Australia and New Zealand. They expected a battle for Australia, but given how ill-prepared New Zealand was to repel an invasion, believed they would have simply occupied this country by phone."

Bram, front row second right, with the 1954 Diploma in
Agriculture intake at Massey University

After graduating from Massey University, Bram completed 50 years service with the Ruakura Agricultural Research Centre in Hamilton and was put in charge of an animal research station at Invercargill. He was fortunate to be awarded a scholarship to study sheep and beef cattle in France. At Ruakura, Bram was also part of a special genetics group which was responsible for sheep and cattle breeding.

In the 1970s and early 1980s the group controlled 14,500 ewes and 5000 beef cattle spread all over New Zealand, mainly on research stations, prison farms, mental health farms, and Landcorp farms. A lot of the work was experimental, and Bram used to travel all over New Zealand.

In 1990, Bram co-authored and published a book with Neil Rennie, a former editor of the *New Zealand Farmer* magazine, called *Livestock Recording for Sheep and Beef,* which went into great detail about how livestock were recorded before the age of electronics.

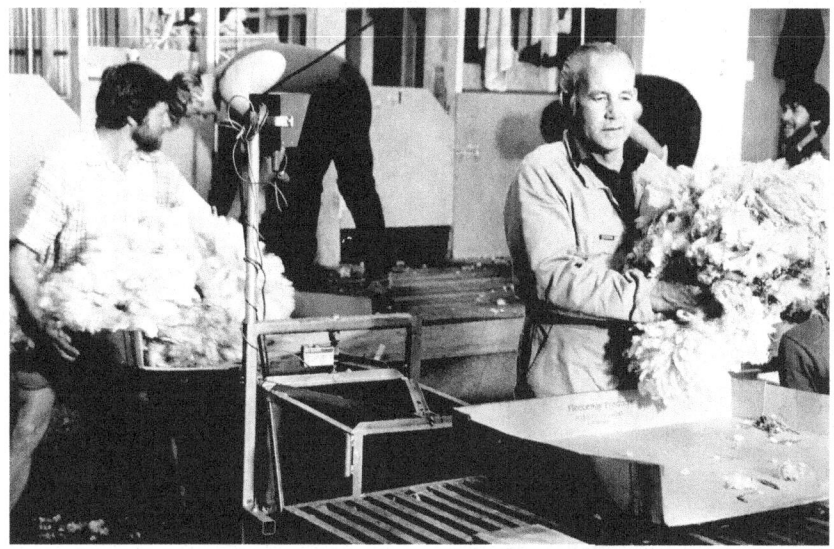

Bram throwing a fleece at the Tokanui Research Station near Te Awamutu, during his work with the Ruakura Agricultural Research Centre.

Another of Bram's jobs at Ruakura was ultrasound scanning of muscles in sheep and beef cattle to determine the muscle area and fat depth.

He was also involved with a group that won several invention awards at the New Zealand National Agricultural Fieldays, the largest event of its type in the Southern Hemisphere, for applying new electronic methods to existing technology.

"I'm quite proud of those achievements. It was all part and parcel of the work we were doing."

Along with having a fulfilling career, Bram had a busy home life, raising three children with his first wife, Evelyn.

Bram still speaks some Indonesian and has returned to the country several times.

"It is always magic to go back to the tea estate, which is still going and run by Indonesians. One of my most treasured possessions is a silver dish, which was presented to my parents the day they were married in 1932 by the 2000 workers on the estate."

The silver dish is engraved with the following words in Indonesian, 'For the lovely bridal couple with many thanks for all you've done for us, from the workers'."

Bram with his first wife Evelyn (seated) and their children (from left) Robyn, Bram Junior and Chris, during the 1980s.

The special family clock

Incredibly, the family's beautiful wooden clock from the tea estate also survived the war.

"We managed to save the clock when our house was burnt down in Bandung. Then one night, before we left Indonesia, the clock was stolen by some thieves who forced entry through the barricades. Dad and I chased them along a small stream, and as luck would have it they dropped the clock, and I heard it chime in the dark. After my parents passed away, the clock was given to me."

The clock takes pride of place on top of the piano, at the home of Bram and his wife Jan, in Te Puke, Bay of Plenty, and is a treasured memento of the past.

Bram said he carried a grudge against the Japanese for many years until the chip on his shoulder 'became a log'. Then he visited the Changi Museum in Singapore, which told the story of the Japanese occupation, and he was able to finally let those feelings go.

"A great sadness came over me as I thought about how grateful I am to all the people who had died so I could be free. Despite the Japanese never apologising for their war crimes, I realised many innocent people had also died under the atom bombs. That's when I knew it was time to forgive. When I left the memorial I felt like I was walking on the moon. A great burden had fallen off me."

Bram and his wife, Jan, on the Sambawa tea estate, left, and with the silver dish presented to his parents on their wedding day in 1932.

O ver the years Bram often wondered what had happened to those three bronzed Australians who had burst out of the jungle and made such an impression on him as a young boy.

"My burning question was – did they make it to Darwin? We heard unconfirmed reports they may have been captured and executed by the Japanese but we never found out for sure."

He did a lot of investigating through the Australian RSL and Canberra War Museum but found no trace of the soldiers.

After a story about Bram and his family was published in the New Zealand *RSA Review* magazine, he was invited to chat with Jim Mora, a host on National Radio, which led to an exciting breakthrough.

"I had emails from people telling me little bits of what they knew, including a chap who told me about a book called *You'll Die in Singapore*, by Charles McCormac who described how he and 16 others broke out of a POW camp in Japanese-occupied Singapore and endured a five month, 2000 mile escape through the jungles of Indonesia to Australia."

The fishing boat in which the men had fled from Singapore was shot up by the Japanese, with the survivors picked up by a Dutch float plane which took them as far as North Sumatra. They travelled the length of Sumatra into West Java where they linked up with some guerillas who were being funded by the Australians. The men were able to hitch a ride back home on an Australian flying boat, which was landing secretly near the West Java coast at night to ferry supplies to the guerillas. Bram was fascinated to read the men's story of courage and endurance, but he wasn't sure if these were the soldiers he had met in West Java until he got to the very last page of the book.

"Right in the back of the book was a map, with dots identifying the trail the escapees had taken. When I saw the dots going right over the top of our tea estate, it was the confirmation I had been looking for. Who knows how different life might have been if we had joined the three Australians on their escape to Darwin? We may have ended up becoming Australian rather than New Zealand citizens? None of the men were still alive by the time I read the book so I wasn't able to make contact with them. However it was fantastic to have closure after all those years wondering about their fate."

2

EVA

IN GERMAN-OCCUPIED ROTTERDAM, in the early 1940s, young Dutch girl, Eva de Konning would set off from her home in the east of the city, and skip over the railway lines towards a German road block.

"Goedemorgen," she would say cheerfully to the German soldiers standing guard, who would return her greeting and wave her through. Eva regularly made the short journey to visit Chris, a barber in the west of the city, and was well known to the soldiers at the roadblock. "Come and sit down Eva," Chris would say on her arrival. "You must be hot. Here, take off your coat. Have some lemonade."

Eva would remove her coat, which had been fashioned from an old blanket, and hand it to Chris. While she drank her lemonade, he would disappear to the back of the barbershop and return a short time later, handing the coat back to Eva. After she had pulled it on over her tiny frame she would start the journey home, passing once more through the roadblock.

This regular routine continued for two or three years. Eva never challenged her father when he said it was time for her to visit Chris at the barbershop. Dirk de Konning was a strict disciplinarian and she followed his instructions without question. Knowing she would get a glass of lemonade or a lolly at the end of the journey, made it worthwhile.

It wouldn't be until after the war that Eva would discover the real purpose of those barbershop visits and find out just how dangerous they really were.

Dirk de Konning (second left) in the early 1900s, with other workers on the farm he would eventually take over from his Uncle Koos (fourth left) and Aunt Kee (sixth left).

Eva de Konning grew up on a large dairy, stock and crop farm on the outskirts of Rotterdam, which was owned by her father, Dirk, a prominent farmer who employed many workers. He would regularly travel throughout Europe on cattle buying and selling trips.

"My father was a gifted stockman and clever businessman who gave us a privileged life. We were well off and brought up with class distinction, which I didn't really like," she said.

Dirk de Konning was born on 8 June 1896 at Maassluis in the western Netherlands, to a Dutch father and French mother. When he was a young boy, he started working for his uncle on the same farm he would eventually take over and run as his own.

"Uncle Koos was stinking rich and would give my father a small amount of money plus food each week for his work. My father spent some of the money buying language dictionaries from second hand shops and managed to teach himself French, Spanish and Portugese while travelling in railcars with my uncle on their various cattle buying trips.

He always said when you can speak another person's language you can do business with them. It meant that later, when the big shots from Europe came to the farm to view the cattle, my father was able to communicate with them."

As a young man, Dirk de Konning fought in World War I but he never believed in war, telling Eva much later it was 'cruel'. She kept his passport from the 1920s, which showed he was a regular visitor to Spain, Italy, France, and other European countries where he bought and sold livestock.

"He was the only person in the Netherlands at the time to have a vee-expeditie (special licence) on his passport allowing him to do his work. He had to be very careful when bringing cattle into the Netherlands not to spread disease and was responsible if something went wrong with the stock."

On his travels, Dirk always carried a photo of his sweetheart, Christine, who worked as a chef for the owner of a large French shipping company.

"My mother was an amazing cook and she didn't use a recipe book. All the recipes were in her head," said Eva.

Like Dirk, Christine came from a large, well off Dutch family. Her grandfather had a thriving business making cigars by hand.

Among Eva's prized possessions were the warm, loving letters and beautiful postcards Dirk sent to her mother during this time. On 4 February 1922 he wrote from Paris, "I'm looking forward to going home so we can welcome each other and have a kiss and a cuddle." On 22 December 1922 he sent a letter from Spain, saying he hoped to be home by Christmas with 40 new cattle. "Barcelona is beautiful. I can't wait to go home. Tell everybody hello and goodbye. I love you and can't tell you that enough. Hope to see one another soon," he wrote.

The devoted couple married in the early 1920s.

Dirk and Christine de Konning on their wedding day.

Eva said her father saw a lot of the world, and was a clever man.

"He said travelling and learning languages gave him the best education."

Dirk gradually took over the farm from his uncle. It was a busy life. As well as running his large farming business employing numerous workers, he and Christine had six children, including Eva, the youngest, who was named after Christine's grandmother, Eva Stoltz, a German woman who had married a Dutchman.

The de Konnings were strong followers of the Catholic faith. Eva and her siblings were taught from a young age to work hard and show respect, particularly to their mother.

"At mealtimes we had to stand up and wait for our mother to sit first. Then everybody else would sit down and we'd say a prayer. My mother would serve her own meal from the dishes on the table before we were allowed to start. We had to respect that she was the cook, so she had to eat first."

Eva always remembered the great love between her parents.

"My sister and I would meet our father at the station when he came back from his cattle buying trips, as he always had some goodies for us. My mother had the most beautiful aquamarine eyes, and when we got home, my father would take her in his arms, kiss her and start to sing an old song, *Two Eyes Ever So Blue*. 'Come on kids, I need a choir,' he would say, and we would all gather around the piano and sing to our mother."

The family's comfortable world was turned upside down on 14 May 1940, when their city was torn apart by the Rotterdam Blitz, a key part of the German invasion of the Netherlands. Relentless bombing destroyed most of the city's heart and sent it into chaos. This led to the Dutch surrender a few days later when the Nazis threatened Utrecht with the same fate. Hundreds of civilians in Rotterdam were killed in the bombing and many young children were orphaned. Around 80,000 people were left homeless.

"When we woke up, the sky was black with planes. Parachutes and bombs rained down and soon the whole city of Rotterdam was on fire. We saw men standing on the roofs of houses with children in their arms, and people screaming as they tried to run to safety outside the city. Many didn't have anywhere else to go. It was terrifying," said Eva.

The de Konnings quickly rallied in the aftermath of the bombing, providing as many people as they could with temporary shelter in their stables. They even took in some of the city's orphaned children.

Aerial view of the destruction of Rotterdam - late
May 1940.

"When we came out of church a week or so after the Blitz, we saw the Red Cross with several children who needed temporary homes until other family members could be found. Among them were three young orphans, named Albert, Harry and Ria, whose parents had been killed. The children had been found huddled together in a bedroom of their bombed house. My mother gave my father a look, which was all it took for him to agree to take them home."

It was a few months before the children's Oma (grandmother) was located. However she was having her own wartime struggles and couldn't afford to look after the children herself.

"There was very little food and people were hungry, but we had enough on the farm. My mother ended up looking after those children for years. After the war the boys found homes with some other relations, but my parents adopted Ria and she became our sister."

The de Konnings took in two other children in need and also some elderly local men who did odd jobs on the farm in return for shelter and food. Eva says their dining table stretched the length of the room to fit the family, their guests and a couple of extra farm workers who also ate with the family each day.

"We had two coal ranges going all the time, cooking meals in big pots as high as the table."

Almost immediately after the invasion, the Germans took over the de Konning's sizeable farm to use as a heavy artillery base, given its strategic location near a dyke and the main railway lines to Utrecht and the city. The farm also had goods train lines crossing its boundary.

The German soldiers took over most of the family's stables for their own horses, with nearly all of the cattle, pigs, milk, eggs and cheese produced on the farm commandeered to feed the German army.

Under the occupation, Rotterdam became split into north, south, east and west zones, which were separated by roadblocks.

"The adults had to show their passports to the soldiers at these roadblocks, but us kids usually went straight through. We already knew most of the German guards at the roadblock closest to the farm, because they lived on our land."

What Eva didn't know at the time was that her father was one of the men leading the Dutch Resistance network in Rotterdam, and he had continued to carry out this dangerous work despite the presence of the Germans.

"He was so secretive about his involvement in the network that even my mother was completely unaware of it. When he went to meetings he would pull on a balaclava and gloves and disguise his voice. People had to be careful not to reveal their faces as someone sitting next to them could be a traitor."

The Dutch Resistance focused mainly on gathering intelligence and rescuing downed Allied airmen. It was essentially a non-violent group, but would carry out occasional acts of sabotage.

Eva said her father personally helped to save the lives of many British and American pilots during the war.

"Big Lancaster bombers used to fly over on their way to Germany but sometimes they would be shot down by the heavy artillery on our land. If the pilots were still alive my father would rescue them and try to help them get back to England."

The usual route was to smuggle the stricken pilots out of Rotterdam, through Schiedam and out to Maassluis where they would be picked up by fishing boats and taken back to England.

Another key role of the local Resistance was to alert the British to locations of war factories in Germany where thousands of young Dutch men had been forcibly requisitioned to make everything from uniforms and munitions, to aircraft.

"The Dutch Resistance worked hard to keep the British informed of where the German factories filled with Dutch men were, as they would otherwise have been prime bombing targets for the RAF. Our farm, with all the German heavy artillery on it, would normally have been a target too, but the British didn't bomb it as they knew it had to be saved for the local Resistance."

Despite living with the enemy, Dirk de Konning bravely continued to send and receive coded messages on his transmitter to contacts in England.

"He would receive important messages about pilots or potential bombing targets that needed to be passed on to members of the Resistance in other parts of Rotterdam. But after the roadblocks went up it was very hard to get messages across the city. Although we had a telephone we couldn't use it because the Germans were so close."

A clever solution had to be found, which led to Eva's regular visits to Chris the barber. She was chosen as a messenger because she was the youngest and fastest runner of the six children in the de Konning family.

"My father used to say, 'Eva, go to the road blocks. Don't stop. Don't talk. Just go to Chris. He is waiting for you and has a lolly.' I didn't realise my father had sewn handwritten notes into the bottom hem of my coat, and while I was enjoying my treat in the barbershop, Chris was out of sight removing the message and replacing it with another for my father."

It wasn't until after the war Eva learned she had been inadvertently working for the Resistance.

"It was incredibly dangerous. If my father or I had been caught they might have shot the whole family. My father said after the war he couldn't have told me what I was really doing because kids talk, but that I was a very brave girl. Even my mother didn't know the truth at the time. When we were growing up my parents always said if you tell a lie you get a black cross on your forehead. But after the war my father said sometimes you are allowed to tell a lie for your own good."

Eva's eldest brother Adrie was also involved in the Resistance but was captured after being recognised by a traitor attending one of the group's meetings. He was sent to a camp in the Netherlands before being moved on to a small concentration camp in Germany in 1943.

The family was devastated. But despite his sorrow at his son's capture, Dirk de Konning's work with the Resistance continued uninterrupted.

"He was determined to keep doing every little thing he could to help."

The family was desperate for news of Adrie but months went by without any word. Eva said as a strong Catholic woman, her mother used to get 'feelings' about things and she would never forget seeing her come down the stairs early on the morning of 5 April 1944 with tears streaming down her face.

"I will always remember the exact date. My mother cried, and cried and cried. I said, 'What happened?' She said 'It's terrible Eva.

Adrie is dead. They took his fingernails and his teeth, and they hit him and hit him to death. I saw it all."

Eva's mother asked her to pray so they clasped hands and knelt down. When her father came in from milking the cows he asked what had happened.

"My mother said, 'Dirk, it's terrible, Adrie is dead. He's lying there dead'. My father told her she must have had a bad dream but she insisted she had seen it all. I was the only one who believed her."

It would be two more years before the family would finally learn Adrie's fate.

E va said her family saw the best and worst of the German people during their wartime experiences.

"We adjusted well to having the German soldiers on the farm. Most of them were farmers from the Rhine, and were good, ordinary men who like so many soldiers on both sides, never wanted to go to war. Thankfully we had no members of the SS or Gestapo on the property."

She remembers one Christmas during the war, when her family went across to the barracks the German soldiers had built in the de Konning's stables, to sing them carols.

"The soldiers had put up a big Christmas tree and were all on their knees, praying to go home."

Eva had treasured wartime photographs of herself and members of her family with some of the German soldiers, including Oscar, who they all grew close to.

"We were very fond of Oscar, who came from a town near Heidelberg and had four children. He was a good man who favoured me because he had a daughter around my age. My mother and I wrote regularly to his mother back in Germany during the war."

Like many of the German soldiers stationed at the de Konning's farm, Oscar was later sent on to the Russian Front.

"He didn't come back. None of them did."

Contrary to the relatively benign presence of the German soldiers on their farm were the atrocities carried out by the Nazis against the Dutch people in Rotterdam.

Eva still carried many terrible images from the war, after witnessing things no young child should ever see.

One day, she and her sister Marie were walking home from piano lessons, passing along a busy thoroughfare next to a train station man wearing a white coat and gloves passed them on a bicycle. Just a few metres away from the girls, he approached a member of the SS, pulled out a revolver and shot him dead.

Eva (third left on the horse), with Harry, a young orphan taken in by her family, brother Theo, and adopted sister Ria, with Oscar the German soldier loved by the family, along with Oscar's horse, Eva's sister Marie (front), brother Adrie and sister Co.

"Marie pulled me to the ground and told me not to look but I did. I saw the SS man lying there dead, and the man who had shot him, jump off his bike, pull off his coat and gloves, and disappear into the crowd. We ran home as fast as we could to tell our mother, and knew we would be in trouble, as we shouldn't have been walking home. Our parents gave us money for the tram, but we were naughty girls and used to walk home so we could use the tram money to buy licorice instead."

Eva also remembered Dutch Jews in the city being 'rounded up like mobs of sheep' and herded onto railway cattle wagons to be transported to the concentration camps.

Eva (right) with her sister Marie.

One day, soon after the German occupation, she and her parents came across a Dutch soldier who had been badly wounded by a grenade.

"They bandaged him as best they could and when my father was getting the horses ready to take him to the nearby hospital he told me to hold my hands tightly over the soldier's wound. My mother prayed over him with her rosary beads and the soldier said 'Is there a God?' 'Of course,' said my mother, you must believe.' The soldier said if she was right and he was still alive a year later he would become a Catholic. We got him to hospital and he survived. True to his word a year later he visited my mother and asked her how to convert."

Towards the end of the war, on 3 April 1945, Eva was horrified to witness a dark day in Rotterdam's history at Oostzeedijk when 20 men were brought before a German firing squad on the side of the dyke at eight o'clock in the morning.

The men were shot in retaliation for the killing of a policeman from Rotterdam who had also been a member of the SS.

"We were running late for Mass and as we came up the steps of the dyke could see a lot of people standing around near a big truck with a canvas back. There were 20 men lined up alongside the dyke who had been taken from every corner of Rotterdam. Then some soldiers, either SS or NSB (a Dutch political party that collaborated with the Germans) came out and shot the men. I couldn't believe what I had seen. It was so horrifying. We couldn't do or say anything, just stand there and keep our mouths shut. We had to be so careful. I'll never forget one of the men. He was wearing a pair of clogs, and after he was murdered his false teeth ended up on his chest."

As the tide eventually turned in the Allies favour, the Germans took several retaliation measures against the Dutch people for acts of resistance, particularly after Dolle Dinsdag, or 'Mad Tuesday' on 5 September 1944.

This celebration occurred the day after the Allies had conquered Antwerp when rumours started to spread about the imminent liberation of the Netherlands. Many Dutch people prepared to receive and cheer the Allies but the joy in some parts of the country was short-lived when the Germans put up a much tougher fight than expected. Soon after Dolle Dinsdag many Dutch people were executed by firing squad for acts of resistance. The Germans also cut off the transport of food and fuel to the larger cities still under occupation.

The lack of food supplies, combined with the worst winter in Europe for years, led to the Dutch famine known as the Hongerwinter (Hunger Winter). Around 4.5 million Dutch people were affected, with soup kitchens playing a big part in their survival. Thousands of people died from malnutrition.

"There was no food. Some tried to cut grass and eat it but it didn't work. People were desperately hungry with some as skinny as the prisoners in the concentration camps. I saw several people drop dead from hunger right in front of me," said Eva.

With the de Konnings forced to feed the German army with their stock and crops, production was allowed to continue on the farm. Eva's father did his best to secretly help those in need.

"We fed so many people but unfortunately couldn't help all of them. My father used to kill a cow or pig on the quiet and take it to the priest and 40 nuns at the parish."

Young Eva would sometimes go with her father to drop milk to the nunnery where the nuns were looking after many unwanted babies.

"I used to like seeing the babies. Their mothers were usually local girls who had taken up with American, Canadian and even German soldiers during the war and became pregnant. They didn't want the babies so dropped them off to the nuns who cared for them until they were old enough to be adopted out to good homes. A lot of them went to Switzerland. Goodness knows how many kids at the end of the war didn't know who their mothers and fathers were."

Eva remembered seeing girls accused of collaborating with the Germans being rounded up by the Dutch Resistance after the war, to undergo public humiliation.

"It was terrible. My father thought it was very wrong, and would say to the men in the Resistance, 'Is that necessary? He said most of them were young girls who had simply fallen in love, or were starving and had sex with a German soldier to get some food."

To help their starving neighbours, nearby Scandinavian countries started to drop biscuits to the Dutch people from the air.

"They also sent bread. We had to queue at the shop and show our passports to receive it. After being without food for so long, people had to be careful not to eat too much, as their stomachs couldn't take it. Some who gorged themselves got very sick or even died."

Dirk de Konning's work with the Resistance continued right up until the end of the war.

"He was still sneaking out at night, going past the heavy artillery and wading through water to a far corner of the farm where he would signal British planes by torchlight so they could safely drop guns for the Dutch Resistance. So many guns arrived on our land and by the end of the war virtually every member of the Resistance had one. My father had to be so careful. His work was incredibly dangerous and the consequences for our family would have been dire had he been caught."

It wasn't until 5 May 1945 that Rotterdam was finally liberated when the Canadians swept into northern and western parts of the Netherlands.

"After the fighting stopped we saw lots of Canadian, British and American soldiers. The tanks rolled into Rotterdam and five minutes later we were on top of them. It was wonderful. We were finally free."

Infantrymen of the West Nova Scotia Regiment in a Universal Carrier en route to Rotterdam, surrounded by Dutch civilians celebrating the liberation of the Netherlands. *Photo: Department of National Defence Library and Archives Canada, PA-134390*

One Sunday afternoon soon after the liberation, Eva and her friend Riet were standing on a dyke watching rail cars filled with Dutch prisoners-of-war and enforced labourers who were being transported back from Germany.

"We were waving and singing and so happy, when all of a sudden Riet yelled, 'Eva, it's your brother, it's Adrie!' I couldn't believe it. He was alive. The rail car was due to stop at another station about five minutes further on, so it was just as well I was a fast runner."

The girls ran to the station and there among all the other men getting off the train was Adrie.

"It was incredible to see him. I said 'Oh my god, you are supposed to be dead', and he said, 'Eva it is a long story'."

The girls walked home with Adrie and found their father milking the cows.

"I said 'Father, come, Adrie is here'. A lot of the farm workers were with him. Nobody could believe it."

Eva's father asked her to go and collect her mother from her Aunt Jul's house, some distance away.

"My mother had a bad heart, so my father said I had to be careful how I told her Adrie was still alive. I ran to my aunt's house and told my mother she had to come home. As we started to walk, I said, 'Mother do you remember the dream where you said Adrie was dead? Well whatever you saw he is not dead. He is at home and he's alive'. She said it was impossible and when we got home she was overcome with emotion. She held Adrie tightly and wouldn't let him go."

Eva said her mother told Adrie about her terrible vision and they were all amazed when Adrie said everything she had seen was true.

"My brother said he had come very close to losing his life after being badly tortured and left for dead by the Gestapo and SS soldiers at the concentration camp. His teeth and fingernails had been removed and his stomach pumped full of water before being jumped on. But despite the cruel torture Adrie still refused to talk. My father used to say once people were tortured they would tell everything. But not Adrie."

At the end of the beating the Germans, thinking Adrie was dead, had thrown him outside among some bodies.

A German farmer, who was at the camp to pick up scraps for his pigs, saw Adrie was still breathing and managed to sneak him onto his truck and take him home.

The kindly farmer and his wife made a bed for Adrie in a farm shed among the animals, as they were too frightened to have him in the house.

"The wife started giving my brother boiled potato water and rice water, because he was almost starved to death and couldn't tolerate solid food. He was also covered in bruises and sores but she did whatever she could to keep him alive. Finally Adrie grew stronger and was able to start eating again. At the end of the war he was finally able to return home."

Eva said the couple who saved Ardrie were highly decorated after the war for their bravery and kindness.

"It was such a big risk. We were so grateful for what they did."

After the war Adrie worked for his father's business. He married, had three children and later wrote about his wartime experiences.

"His health wasn't one hundred per cent for the rest of his life. He had high blood pressure and died of cancer at the age of 71."

———

After the war, life slowly returned to normal for the de Konnings. With their large farm, substantial stabling, and the 30 houses they owned in Rotterdam to accommodate their farm workers, the family was able to make good extra money hosting horses and riders participating in the Concours Hippique International Officiel horse riding competition in Rotterdam, which by the end of the 1940s had grown into an international event.

"We had horses and people come and stay for a couple of weeks from right throughout Europe, including Belgium, Germany, Norway, Sweden, Turkey and England."

One year the family looked after the horses of Prince Bernhard of the Netherlands, the consort of Queen Juliana.

"I told the Prince I had been looking after his horses, and he said 'Young madam, thank you very much, but don't make them too fat."

During the riding events, Eva's mother would empty out the farmhouse the family used for butter and cheese making, and set up a restaurant to feed the guests.

"My parents did very well out of it. It was my job to collect the money off everyone."

The painting by Eva's Uncle Koos.

Christine de Konning's brother Koos, who was an artist, would sometimes visit the family, staying for a few weeks at a time, said Eva.

"My uncle never married, and lived like a homeless person, travelling all over Europe selling his paintings. When he visited, my mother would buy him clothes and shoes and look after him until it was time for him to leave again. During one visit he did a painting of part of our farm."

With the German presence gone from the property, Dirk de Konning was able to continue running his large-scale business, with Eva his enthusiastic apprentice.

"My father started to travel throughout Europe again, buying and selling cattle. We always had lots of stock to unload from the railway. I loved it. I would sit glued to my father's lap as he told me about the cows and their history. I knew all about their breeding and how to inject good blood into the herd from the best steers and bulls. My father had a room full of papers with information about every cow."

Eva also loved going to the weekly cattle markets with her father. On Monday mornings the family's drovers would take a selection of 50–70 of their best beef cattle to a market attended by Rotterdam's top butchers.

Dirk de Konning (in suit and tie) with some of his farm workers in the 1940s.

The following day, the de Konnings would drive an additional 300 cattle through the city to the Grote Markt, which at the time was the biggest weekly market in the Netherlands.

"People used to come from as far away as France to look at all the breeding stock."

When Eva was in her early teens, Dirk De Konning told her he was putting her in charge of selling the cattle they were offering at the market that day.

"He said, 'I know you can do it. Sell them all together and we need to get at least 750 guilders for every cow.' Then he disappeared into the crowd."

Eva was shaking as the buyers approached. The first buyer asked her the price and she told him 850 guilders.

"He said you'll have to come down and although I came down a bit, he said no and walked away. I started all over again with another buyer and the same thing happened. When I realised I was asking too much I decided to offer the next buyer 800 guilders. But no one came. I remember thinking I couldn't take those cattle home."

Finally, one last buyer did come along. He asked Eva where her father was and she told him he was on the other side of the market but she could sell the cows to him for 800 guilders.

"The buyer said that was too much, so I said, 'Come on, look at these cows. They have good calves, good udders, good milk and are in good order.' He told me he would only put in one bid take it or leave it, so I asked him what he was prepared to offer. He said 780 guilders. I clapped my hands together and said, sold. I was so proud. I felt 10 feet tall."

The deal was put in writing and when Dirk de Konning returned, he was delighted to find Eva had made the sale.

"My father was so pleased and said he would stay at home next time and leave the selling to me. He gave me so much confidence. I found out much later he had told many people about me selling the cattle."

After the success of Eva's first big sale, it wasn't long before she was regularly in charge of selling cattle for the family business. While working alongside her father she also learned how to care for their stock. With not too many vets in those days, Dirk de Konning carried out most of the animal health tasks on the farm himself.

"My father learned everything he knew from his uncle, and had almost as much experience as a vet."

She remembered one occasion when one of their best breeding cows was having trouble calving.

"My father could see the calf was twisted inside her. He rang the vet and told him he would get the cow ready to be operated on. I was allowed to come because I was Miss Important. He spread some white cotton sheets around the cow and took some long instruments from his bag, which was of similar size to a golf bag. Then he stripped off half naked and disinfected everything. He knew the calf was dead and would have to be cut out in pieces, so he got to work."

By this time, the vet and some students had arrived, and were watching Eva's father. Once he removed the calf he put the pieces out on a white sheet and checked everything was there before stitching up the cow.

"His biggest worry was the afterbirth coming out. He made up a mixture, which had ginger and alcohol in it, and put it in a bottle with a long neck. I had to give it to the cow morning, afternoon and night and keep her warm with horse blankets. The afterbirth did eventually come out and the cow recovered. I remember after it was all finished I was allowed to go to the shop and get a salty drop lolly."

Eva also learned how to calve cows at her father's side, and was later put in charge of this when he was away on his regular trips to France, Germany and Belgium.

"My father gave me a wooden stick with a grip and string attached, which I would tie around the back legs of a calf as it was being born, if the mother was in trouble. He taught me how to pull when the cow pushed, and then ease off again. On the third pull, the calf would usually come out. However it was much harder if the calf was breech and its front legs came out first."

When calves were born, Dirk de Konning would ensure they had one good drink of colostrum from their mothers. Then he would harvest the rest of the colostrum to give to the local hospital for sick people and pregnant women.

"Colostrum from cows was known as the 'beast' in the Netherlands and was said to be very good for people's systems."

Eva said the family's entire operation was put at risk when a new cow arrived on the property with foot and mouth disease.

If word had got out, their whole herd would have been slaughtered and burned, and all the hard work they had put into their breeding programme would have gone to waste.

"When my father bought new cows he always looked into their mouths with a torch to check for disease, but he must have overlooked this one. He told me he was going to make the cow healthy again and he needed me to help him. But I had to keep it a secret just between us, otherwise we could lose all our cows. Even Adrie couldn't know."

The cow was locked in a little stable, way down the end of the farm.

"She was standing on sacks and we had to keep her in the pitch dark. I would go into the stable with my torch and feed her lots of oats and greens, and a mixture my father made himself which had things like molasses, ginger, garlic and some type of alcohol, possibly cognac in it. We had to take her temperature and test samples of what came out of her backside. It took about five or six weeks, but my father and I cured her in that stable in the dark."

Eva said she learned so much from her father, whose philosophy was to 'never be frightened, just do it, and never look back over your shoulder'. She loved that her father demonstrated such trust in her.

"I loved the farm, and I loved him. We were very close."

———

When she was just 14 years old, Eva met and fell in love with Johannes (John) Van Mulken, the man who would eventually become her husband.

"My girlfriend Riet and I were standing in front of a shop window in Rotterdam looking at watches and rings, when all of a sudden these two sailors were behind us asking if we wanted to go to the pictures. We already had tickets, so I said 'why not?'. It was dark when we went into the theatre and both John and his friend wanted to sit next to me, but John pushed his friend away. After the film we walked over to the trams together and as we waited for Riet and John's friend to catch up, he looked at me, held both my hands, and said, 'You're a lovely girl. Would you like to marry me?' I said yes, and that's how it started."

It was close to Eva's fifteenth birthday when they started dating and romance quickly blossomed.

The smitten young couple used to meet secretly at a café on the other side of the railway tracks from where Eva and her sister Marie had seen the member of the SS gunned down during the war.

"John would have a beer, I would have a croquette and a coffee and we would talk for about an hour. I told my mother about John after we had met a few times and she said he had better be a Catholic, because otherwise I wasn't to bother bringing him home. She was so religious."

To the left of the station is the cafe where Eva and John would secretly meet. To the right is where Eva and Marie witnessed the killing of the member of the SS.

Eva said the conversation with John about religion came up when she mentioned a film called *The White Nun*, which was showing in Rotterdam.

"I said to John I'd heard it was a beautiful film, and that my family was Catholic, was his? He said 'Of course. I come from Limburg and we're all Catholic down there.' I was so pleased as religion ruled your life in those days."

On the day of their wedding Eva's mother said, 'I know there is a reason you are getting married so young but I just can't see it '.

"Two years later she was dead at the age of 54 following a heart attack. I cried for two solid years but at least I was in my place with a lovely husband. That was the reason."

Eva said she learned the important things in life from her mother.

"We were always taught to help people, especially during the war when we were giving people food and had all those extra people living in the house. She used to say giving was much better than taking and love was the most important thing. I was lucky to find love when I was very young. And the day I married the man I loved, I became a free woman."

Eva and Johannes (John) Mulken on their wedding day.

The happy young couple moved to Maastricht and within three weeks of their wedding conceived their first child.

Just one month later, John was called up to serve for the Dutch Navy in the Indonesian Freedom War, where Dutch colonialism was coming to a brutal end.

"Because I was pregnant I went back to stay with my parents, who were so busy and needed another pair of hands in the business. I helped my mother to cook and clean. We would ring a special bell to let the men know it was morning and afternoon tea time, and I used to cook soup for them. I loved it."

The family's accountant would work out all the wages for the drovers, then Eva would go to the bank, collect the money and fill the pay packets ready for pay day every Saturday morning.

She also used to organise the drovers to drive the cattle to and from the market, and if she couldn't find enough people, would sometimes go herself. However her mother soon put a stop to that, given she was pregnant. John missed Eva's entire pregnancy, as well as the birth of their son John in Rotterdam. Eva's father went with her into the city to register the birth.

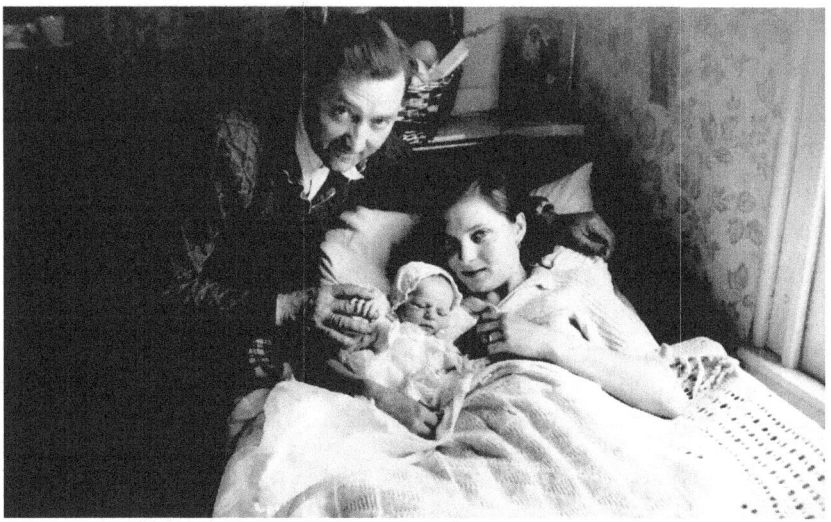

Eva with her father and newborn son, John.

"I was so worried about John during the war, and hoped and prayed he would come home. I was so lucky he did, as a lot of his friends didn't make it, including the friend who had been with us at the pictures on the night we met. John told me some of the awful things he experienced in the war. It was terrible," she says.

The couple's son, John was around 18 months old when he saw his father for the first time. Eva said their daughter Christina was conceived the day John arrived back from the war. By the early 1950s, work was becoming scarce in the Netherlands and the couple struggled to find enough work to support themselves.

"I wouldn't have minded moving back with John's parents as they were good people who I could trust. However there wasn't enough for me to do. At the time there was strong Dutch migration to New Zealand, so we decided to move there to look for new opportunities."

Some time later, Adrie took over the family farming business from Dirk de Konning, but it was impossible for him to live up to the reputation of his father. He also had his own struggles to deal with, given what he had suffered during the war.

"My father used to tell me Adrie was good, but I was more like him, and could have taken the farm over. But Adrie was a man and that's how things worked in those days. I wasn't disappointed. I told my father I didn't need it anyway."

Eva was in her early twenties when she and her family arrived in New Zealand with little money or possessions.

"We never looked over our shoulders. We decided to give it two years and if we didn't like it we'd move back home. But we loved it."

The couple settled in Greymouth, on the West Coast of the South Island, where John worked on the railway for two years and Eva went nursing at Greymouth Hospital. However business ran in Eva's blood, and she was determined the couple should do something for themselves.

"We borrowed some money from the bank, moved to Christchurch and started a cafe called the Blue Mill Milk Bar in the suburb of Sydenham."

It wasn't long before the hardworking couple had transformed the five-day-a-week business into a seven-day operation, which opened at 6am each morning.

"We were the first people in Christchurch to sell coffee made in percolators we brought out from the Netherlands. We'd sell the first cup for eight-pence, and the second and third cups for free. All the carriers in Christchurch used to come into the nice warm shop for a coffee and some good food like savouries and toasties. I used to make other food using my mother's recipes."

Soon the Mulkens were selling chocolates, books and newspapers from the shop, which quickly became a success, said Eva.

"It was a real goldmine but we didn't overcharge or lose sight of the things we had learned during the wars. When my husband was in Indonesia he never forgot how the Salvation Army used to give the soldiers parcels and magazines. He insisted that when Salvation Army members from Christchurch came into the milk bar on Friday afternoons they wouldn't have to pay for their tea. Sometimes we'd be making free tea for 10, 12 or 14 people but it didn't matter."

Eva and John outside the Blue Mill Milk Bar.

The Mulkens were repaid one Christmas by 'one of most beautiful things' Eva ever saw.

"One Friday afternoon before Christmas, the entire Salvation Army Band came to play in front of our shop to say thank you. The business people next door were saying, 'What have you got that we haven't'?' We said, love in life and helping people, the most important things."

Eva was devastated to lose her husband John, a longtime smoker, to cancer in 1994.

"He was a good man and the love of my life. There was so much love between us that I can't describe it. We were always together, happy, singing and dancing. Money didn't rule our life. Love did."

Father Anton, a Catholic priest from Oamaru, who officiated at John's funeral service told Eva she had suffered a big loss.

"I said, 'Father, when I came out to New Zealand in the 1950s with my husband and two beautiful children in my arms we had nothing, but I was the richest woman in this world. Then we got houses, we got land and I had all the material things I wanted, but I have no husband, so now I'm the poorest'."

A Mulken family portrait painted a few years after they
arrived in New Zealand.

In 2010, Eva's adopted home city of Christchurch, in the South Island of New Zealand, was hit by the first of a series of devastating earthquakes. A 6.3 magnitude shake on 22 February 2011 caused widespread destruction and 185 people lost their lives.

More than 1000 commercial buildings were pulled down in the city centre along with thousands of homes in the wider suburbs. It would be many years before these gaps are completely filled. Eva's home in the suburb of Riccarton was broken but liveable throughout the thousands of aftershocks endured by the city's residents.

Like many others in Christchurch and the surrounding Canterbury region, Eva's insurance negotiations took years, and it wasn't until mid-2017, more than six years after the big quake, that she was able to finalise matters and the house was demolished.

Eva said it was an unbelievable coincidence to see her two home cities endure such devastation.

"All those years ago I saw Rotterdam razed to the ground and rebuilt. Now the same thing had happened in Christchurch. I never imagined I'd experience something like that twice in a lifetime."

Eva with some her treasures, including precious family photographs, the bell, rosary beads and special cross.

A large collection of photographs, letters, her father's rosary beads and the bell from their farm at Rotterdam were among Eva's cherished treasures, which helped to keep the precious memories of her beloved family, and particularly her husband John, alive.

Despite the heartbreak, the challenges she faced, and atrocities she witnessed, Eva's zest for life was undiminished. She continued to be philosophical about the lessons her family, and her life experiences had taught her.

"I have seen so much. But I have been able to cope with it by focusing on the important things my mother taught me - helping others, and love, the most important of all to me."

3

NAYLOR

UNTIL HE WAS ALMOST 100 years old, Flying Officer Naylor Hillary, NZ423918, didn't reveal his top secret wartime service, even to his family.

He didn't wear his medals during Anzac Day celebrations each year to avoid having to answer questions about where and with whom he had served. It wasn't until early 2015, when Naylor's family in New Zealand was preparing for his 100th birthday that his daughter Pam Bissland asked if he had any photographs of himself as a young man, which they could use to create a display.

Naylor went into his bedroom and came back with a shoebox containing several images. One photograph showed him resplendent in his flight kit about to head off on a mission with the RAF crew he had served with during World War II. His son-in-law, David Biss-land, asked if he could remember the names of the men in the photo, and Naylor told him every one, apart from the surname of the engineer, whose first name was Johnny. David offered to search for Johnny's surname on the internet and asked Naylor for his squadron number so he could look it up.

Naylor told David he was in Royal Air Force (RAF) 138 Squadron, but he wouldn't be able to find any information about it, because it was top secret. That evening, David went online and came across a web page set up by Bob Body, who had also published a book called *Runways to Freedom* about the 138 and 161 Special Duty Squadrons. They had flown out of RAF Tempsford, Churchill's most important secret airfield.

"As I read through the information on Bob's website I was amazed to discover Naylor was part of a crew flying Stirling Mark IV planes on clandestine supply and agent delivery missions into enemy occupied Europe," said David.

Naylor was unaware that the wartime activities at Tempsford Airfield had been released from the Official Secrets List decades earlier, and had steadfastly maintained his silence about his work there during the war. David made contact with Bob Body, also a founder member of the Tempsford Veterans and Relatives Association (TVARA), who was pleased to learn of a new living Tempsford veteran.

"Bob phoned me from his home in Greece, gave me Johnny's surname, and later emailed all the operational records from Naylor's crew to me. We printed them out and gave them to Naylor on his 100th birthday."

Naylor was also presented with a large birthday card, signed and sent by TVARA members who had gathered a month earlier at Tempsford for their annual get together. Lady Erroll, the owner of Gibraltar Farm Estate, where Tempsford Airfield was based during World War II had also signed the card. A video of the group singing *Happy Birthday* to Naylor was also sent to New Zealand.

"It was really special," said David.

Just before Christmas 2016, Naylor was awarded the National Order of the Legion of Honour (Légion d'Honnéur) by the President of the French Republic for his actions on those top secret missions during World War II. He received the medal from the Honorary French Consul in Christchurch, Martine Marshall-Durieux. The citation read, 'Our country wishes to honour the bravery you demonstrated with the highest decoration that exists in France'.

He was delighted, although in typical humble fashion, wasn't sure about being singled out, and said, "it wasn't just me, it was all of my crew".

Serving God and country was always foremost in Naylor's mind during his wartime service, and he carried out both with distinction.

The Hillary family in 1922, (from left) Barbara, Naylor's mother
Annie, Mavis, Naylor, his father John and Joan.

Naylor George Hillary was born in Christchurch, New Zealand on 17 July 1915, the youngest of four children.

His family was quite comfortably off, as his father John was an urban valuer and partner in a successful real estate firm in the city called Hillary and Baxter. The family lived in a large villa in the suburb of Opawa. They had their own tennis court and spent idyllic summers at their holiday house at Diamond Harbour, a small settlement opposite the city's main port of Lyttelton.

One of Naylor's earliest memories was of his father bringing one of the first Dodge motorcars into New Zealand from America.

"It was my father's first car, as he had ridden a motorcycle with sidecar before that. The garage was too small for the new Dodge and shortly after my father bought it, he drove the car a bit too far in and knocked the end wall out of the garage onto the glasshouse. That was the end of the glasshouse and I remember being rushed into the house. At least we got a new garage out of it," he said.

Naylor (extreme right) playing a tennis match at St Andrew's College, Christchurch in 1929.

Naylor's three sisters, Barbara, Mavis and Joan were all privately educated at Rangi Ruru Girls' School, where Barbara and Joan were prefects, and Mavis was Dux and Head Prefect. She later worked as a nursing matron at Timaru Hospital, with Barbara becoming a Karitane and Plunket Nurse, caring for babies, young children and their mothers. Naylor, who was younger by quite a few years, went to Opawa School, and completed his secondary education at St Andrew's College, a private Presbyterian Boys' School, although he was, and remained throughout his life, a committed Methodist.

"I was very involved in Bible Class as a youngster. The teachings we had there gave us the real bones of Christianity. I accepted it into my life early and never rebelled against. I always felt the need to worship somewhere. I even met my wife Ida in a church, in England, during the war," he said.

After leaving school, Naylor was offered the opportunity to join the National Bank as a cadet, which he accepted.

After working in a Christchurch branch for a time, he was transferred to Timaru, a small city around two hours further south.

"I lived on the bank premises in Timaru for several years, with one of my jobs being to protect the bank. I had to sleep with a revolver under my pillow. I never practised so don't know what I would have done if I'd had to use it. Thankfully I never had to find out."

In 1937, Naylor went to work for his father's firm, Hillary and Baxter, which had offices at 178 Manchester Street, in a building constructed by the firm around the time of his birth, and which stood for almost 100 years, until it was demolished after the Christchurch earthquakes of 2010 and 2011.

Naylor was working in Christchurch when war broke out in 1939.

As a committed churchman, he thought long and hard about whether to enlist.

"War is never an easy thing. When I left New Zealand the threat from the Japanese was very evident. I thought highly of the men who were prepared to stand up and say no – pacifists who said they would not go. I wrestled with that for a long time but decided that it had to be. There is a certain evil in the world and unfortunately there always will be."

Naylor signed up for the New Zealand Army in 1940, did his

training, and was kitted out to go overseas. Then it was discovered he would have to be discharged out of the army for medical reasons. To prove he had volunteered, he was given a V lapel badge. Later, in 1942, he was declared medically fit, which coincided with the Royal New Zealand Air Force having a big recruitment drive. Naylor enlisted with them at the age of 27.

Naylor's RNZAF Identity Card

On 20 May 1942 he commenced training at Harewood, in Christchurch, and was posted to the North Island that September, where he was based at both New Plymouth and Rotorua. On 1 April 1943 he embarked for Canada by ship, to join the Commonwealth Training Scheme.

"We were sent to No. 5 AOS Winnipeg to do our main training. I hadn't been in a plane at all until I arrived at Winnipeg. I was airsick the first five times I flew, however, I eventually got used to it and was still able to do the work."

In Canada, Naylor commenced training as an Air Observer, but was remustered to Navigator (Special).

"It was something I was interested in. My strongest point as far as education was concerned was mathematics, which stood me in good stead."

He learned to navigate by DR, or dead reckoning, which is the process of calculating one's current position by using a previously determined position, and advancing that position based on known or estimated speeds over elapsed time and course. Identifying landmarks on the ground was another key aspect of this highly complex navigation work, which could be thrown off by several factors such as wind.

"During training we learned the effects of the wind pushing us off course and how to adjust for that. This would prove vital for our work later on."

After several months in Canada, Naylor was sent to Britain, arriving on 2 December 1943.

He spent a short period in Brighton, before being sent to the No. 2 Observer, Advanced Flying Unit at Millom Air Base, in Cumberland, where he spent two months undertaking advanced training and getting used to the different flying conditions in England. One Sunday, while in Millom, he attended a local Methodist church, where members of the parish would often invite airmen attending a service, home for an afternoon of rest, relaxation and home cooking.

"I went along, and met a young woman named Ida Penny, who invited me home for lunch. We started a friendship and I saw a bit of her when I was stationed at Millom. After that I would visit her when I could."

After Millom, Naylor was moved to the No. 11 Operational Training Unit (OTU) at Westcott and Oakley, where on 14 March 1944, he met the crew who would play such an important role in his life over the next 18 months.

Naylor was one of a large group at the OTU, which spent a couple of days mingling in the mess room. The men didn't realise they were being observed and assessed by the pilots, who were deciding which airmen to approach for their crews. A highly-skilled young Welsh pilot, Flight Sergeant Doug Banbury, eventually asked Naylor to be his navigator. The rest of the crew included three Englishmen, Johnny Harland (engineer), Bunny Austin (gunner), and George Anderson (dispatcher); along with two fellow Kiwis, Ray Price (radio), and Ray Jorgenson (air bomber).

Naylor and the other navigators were introduced to radar, a revolutionary new technology, which the RAF had integrated as part of the National Air Defence early in the war.

"The radar covered the whole of England and a certain distance beyond its shores. Once you mastered it, you could be sure of your position at any time."

On 29 April 1944, Naylor was promoted to Flight Sergeant, and within days the crew made its first flight together in a twin-engine Wellington aircraft.

"With the second front underway, we were on standby for the landings at Normandy in case we were needed to fly over and drop what they called silver paper, which disturbed the radar of the enemy. However they didn't need us to fly in the end."

In July, the crew was transferred to the 1651 Heavy Conversion Unit at Wratton Common where they converted from the two-engine Wellingtons to Stirlings.

These were the first four-engined heavy bombers introduced into service by the RAF, with the purpose of improving strategic bombing capability. The Stirling was designed by Short Brothers, which had designed and was building the Sunderland military flying boat, already famous during World War II. This experience helped the company to secure a contract with the British government to build the Stirling.

On 9 July 1944, Naylor's crew took a Stirling Mark I out on circuits and landings training, and just two days later had their first flight in a Stirling Mark III. Soon after they were offered the chance to do low level, cross-country training, which they began on 19 July 1944.

"We didn't know exactly what the purpose of the low level flying was, but Doug the skipper was keen on it and the rest of us agreed and were quite happy about it too. We thought it might be in preparation for Coastal Command work, dropping bombs on submarines or something like that, but it turned out to be much more exciting."

Naylor's crew (from left) Bunny Austin (gunner), Naylor Hillary (navigator), George Anderson (dispatcher), Ray Price (radio), Doug Banbury (skipper), Johnny Harland (engineer) and Ray Jorgenson (air bomber).

A few weeks later, Naylor and his crew were transferred to the small rural hamlet of Tempsford in Bedfordshire. They joined the RAF No. 138 (Special Duties) Squadron, which had a crest incorporating the motto 'For Freedom', featuring a sword slicing through a Gordian knot, symbols reflecting freedom from bondage.

The 161 Squadron was also based at Tempsford, and between them the squadrons flew a mixed bag of aircraft, large Stirlings and

Halifaxes, the Lockheed Hudson (a twin engine bomber) and the single engine Lysander.

Finally, the true nature of their work at Tempsford was revealed to Naylor's crew. During a brief, they learned they would be carrying out top secret missions, supporting various Resistance forces operating throughout Western Europe.

"The main mission of 138 Squadron was to fly by moonlight, and sneak under the radar into Nazi occupied countries to drop in agents, operators, and supply the various Resistance movements with supplies. We were sworn to secrecy, security was incredibly tight, and we were told in no uncertain terms we couldn't say anything to anyone about our work, wherever we were."

RAF Tempsford Airfield was built in 1940 on 500 acres of land known as Tempsford Flats in the parish of Everton in Bedfordshire. It had three concrete runways, each of around 1300 yards in lengths, two of which were later extended to almost 2000 yards to meet the requirements of the Special Operations Executive (SOE).

The SOE had been set up by the British government in 1940 to conduct espionage, sabotage and reconnaissance in occupied Europe, and later conducted missions into France, Belgium, Holland, Denmark, Poland and Norway.

Other participants of the secret operation at Tempsford were the UK Secret Intelligence Service (MI6), the Free French Bureau Central de Renseignements et d'Action, the US Office of Strategic Services (OSS), and the Soviet NKVD.

The highly dangerous, clandestine missions flown by the 138 Squadron and 161 Squadron took place during a period of about a week each side of the full moon.

The planes flew without lights or radar, with the moonlight enabling the crews to navigate using features on the ground.

This led to them becoming known as the 'Moonlight Squadrons'. Hitler was said to have referred to them as the 'Nest of Vipers'.

Naylor's skills as a navigator would prove paramount when flying in such tricky conditions. His role was considerably more demanding than that of a navigator on a normal bomber, as the target was not a large city, railway or dock, but a tiny field in the countryside, or perhaps a mountain valley.

"It was all dead reckoning navigation, and we didn't have much to go on. We only worked two weeks each month during the moon period because it was essential for us to see the ground we were passing over without using radar," he said.

The 138 Squadron was based at Tempsford Airfield from March 1942, with the 161 Squadron arriving a month later. Large hangars were built at the airfield and various buildings at the adjacent Gibraltar Farm, on the eastern perimeter of the airfield, were converted into high security SOE stores, an agent reception area, and pre-flight preparation centre. Container packing facilities were organised close to the nearby town of St Neots. A local manor house near the airfield was taken over and set up as the senior RAF officers' mess and sleeping quarters. The house was also the last stopover for the SOE agents before they were driven to the barn at Gibraltar Farm to prepare for their flights.

Tempsford Airfield became associated with some of the war's most highly decorated agents such as Peter Churchill, Violette Szabo (who aged just 23 was captured, tortured and executed by the Nazis), Nancy Wake (known as the 'White Mouse' who was born in New Zealand, grew up in Australia and by 1943 was the Gestapo's most wanted person), Andrée Borrel, Lise de Baissac, and Wing Commander Yeo-Thomas (known as 'The White Rabbit').

They were among almost 1000 brave agents and operators spirited out of Tempsford by the courageous flight crews during operations.

In July 1944, just before Naylor's crew arrived at Tempsford, the 138 Squadron converted from Halifax aircraft to a specially adapted Stirling Mark IV, a modified version of the Stirling Mark III bomber they had trained in at Wratton Common.

The nose gun was removed to provide better vision for the bomb aimer, who in 138 Squadron, acted as the second navigator. He was seated in the nose of the aircraft and with a clear view of the terrain, it was part of his job to call out the landmarks to Naylor as they approached.

The mid upper gun turret was also removed, with the gunner becoming a dispatcher instead. His job was to push supplies and agents out of the 'Joe Hole' or large trap door in the floor.

The cargo might contain anything from arms, ammunition, wireless equipment and food, to clothing, medical supplies, and even pigeons.

"Whatever the agents needed, we tried to fly over to them," said Naylor.

Naylor's crew and ground crew, with a Stirling Mark VI at Tempsford.

Some of the items were packed into large cylinders capable of holding around 220 pounds of weight each, which were carried in the Stirling's bomb bays. Other heavier equipment, such as bicycles and bicycle tyres for the French, and skis and sleighs for the Norwegians, were attached to parachutes and carried inside the aircraft ready to be pushed out by the dispatcher.

Naylor said the Stirling Mark IV was well equipped for navigation work.

"The chair was a high back office chair and there was plenty of room on the table for working. Rather unlike a Lancaster where I had to sit on a bare stool."

Training in low level flying continued for Naylor's crew when they first arrived at Tempsford. The area was very flat and they practised hedgehopping, or coming down to tree level and just rising up over the top.

"I'm afraid we must have scared the life out of a lot of farmers and animals, who would have been shocked to see a four-engine bomber flying at such a low height. But the training was needed for the pilots."

Naylor's crew didn't have the most auspicious start with 138 Squadron, when flying their first three missions between 9–14 August 1944.

They flew in Halifax and Oxford aircraft rather then their usual Stirling, and had three different skippers, instead of Flight Sergeant Banbury.

While carrying out their first war operation into France, where they dropped five containers, nine packages and 20 pigeons, the aircraft was damaged after clipping a tree during low level flying.

"We came back to Tempsford with a tree branch stuck in the wing, so a new wing had to be put onto the aircraft. We weren't very popular. On the next trip, which was a local exercise, we came back with a very large seabird in the wing, which had to be changed again. It wasn't the best start."

By 15 August 1944, Doug Banbury was skipper again, and by the time they completed their first war operation as a crew to France on 28 August, Naylor was learning just how critical his training on dead reckoning would prove.

"The big bombers flew much higher than us, and had additional radar assistance, but once we left the English radar system, we were on our own, a lone plane in the night sky relying entirely on observing where we were. A lot depended on the navigator being able to pinpoint landmarks, and fix our position at any one time, so that alterations in the wind could be adjusted immediately. The wind was a major factor when plotting the course, as you had to correct for it to get a direct line to the target."

The barn at Gibraltar Farm, where the agents were kitted out before their missions.

Any agents being spirited out of Tempsford, were kitted out in the barn at Gibraltar Farm before the flights, with parachutes and other equipment such as suitcase radios. Final checks would be made to ensure none of their clothing had British labels or they were carrying anything else to betray their identities. The agents were often issued with suicide pills to save themselves from torture should they be captured. Naylor says the crew had little contact with the many agents they dropped behind enemy lines.

"We weren't allowed anywhere near the barn, and the only crew member who got to meet them personally was our dispatcher, who had been specially trained to look after them."

The target for each operation was a pre-determined location, generally a clearing in the wood or an open field, where the aircraft would drop agents from about 700 feet, and supplies from around 450 feet. With no fighter escort for their missions, Naylor's crew often had to contend with flak and fighter defences.

Escape photos, buttons that formed a compass, and a tiny compass hidden inside a pencil were special supplies given to Naylor's crew in case they were shot down.

"We quickly discovered that once we were through the defences we could rise to a reasonable height to make it easier to map read across the countryside and get to the right height to make the drop."

Landmarks such as rivers, roads and railways were critical to the navigation.

The only help from the ground was torchlight, with the brave men and women of the Resistance flashing a pre-arranged letter signal in Morse Code, and arranging themselves into a pattern to indicate the dropping or landing zone.

"As we came to the zone, the bomb bay doors were opened and the canisters released by parachute. Other goods inside the aircraft were tossed out attached to parachutes, to hopefully land as close as possible to the reception committee."

Sometimes the planes were prevented from reaching the target due to bad weather or enemy fire. Wind yet again, was another challenge, as if packages were blown too far from the drop zone and found by the Germans, an entire local district could be put at risk of the Gestapo's scrutiny.

"Not every drop was successful. If we got to a site and the torch signal was wrong or we had any doubts about the people on the ground, we just turned around and went back with our load."

Once an operation was completed at the drop zone, Naylor would plot the course for their return, avoiding known fighter stations and areas where there was a lot of defensive flak. The concentration required to complete these sorties was immense.

Members of the Resistance collecting supplies dropped by parachute.

The work carried out by 138 Squadron was so secret that even Naylor's crew didn't discuss the actual locations of the operations amongst themselves.

This was a much different set up from a normal bomber squadron, where its 25 or so crews would get together for a joint briefing before a big bombing raid. At Tempsford, each crew was briefed individually about their missions, and didn't share the information with other crews in the squadron.

"Although we were all airmen living on the base together it was a difficult situation as crews were taking off at different times, and doing such secret work we couldn't discuss where we'd been or why. The 138 Squadron had separate quarters from the crews in the 161 Squadron. They did more of the quick pickup work, landing behind enemy lines in smaller Lysander aircraft to collect people who needed to escape or to return to England with vital information."

Naylor said his crew was very close, and slept in the same huts, apart from the officers.

"They would come over to our huts to socialise but we couldn't go to theirs."

A typical day at Tempsford depended on whether or not Naylor's crew was on 'ops'. The day started when the list of crews required for the coming night was posted on a board outside the office. If Naylor's crew were flying they would attend a brief, which took place a few hours before takeoff.

"The pilots were included in a second brief with the navigators when the actual targets were disclosed and the general conditions for the night were discussed, with the type of weather likely to be met and amount of cloud and so on. Then the navigators were briefed individually about a suggested route to the target, including the possibility of meeting enemy opposition on the way and how to avoid that."

Navigators, like Naylor, were the hardest working members of each crew. After the briefing they were issued with a map of the area where they were flying, and a vague chart to enable them to plot their course.

"It was necessary to work out each individual leg of the course, as well as the compass readings for the pilot, both to the target and for the way back."

Once the brief was concluded there was a short time available to relax before takeoff. From there, the navigator would take over the directions the plane was to fly.

If there were no operations on a particular day, the crew's time was more or less its own. Naylor enjoyed visiting churches in nearby villages where he met a number of local families. For many years after the war he exchanged Christmas cards with a couple he met in Tempsford, and later in his life continued to correspond with their daughter, who still lived in the village.

He said the crew had a 'very happy' time at Tempsford and the nearby village of Everton, which had a pub that was popular with some of the airmen. The journey back to base included a downhill cycle, with a sharp bend at the bottom, where several of Naylor's colleagues came adrift as they returned late at night after a few drinks. The Station Commander threatened to put any airman on defaulters who reported in sick due to not taking the bend.

With their flight schedule dictated by the moon, Naylor's crew had a fortnight's leave each month, which was different to a normal bomber squadron. They were required to spend one week on station, but were free to travel during the second week.

"We were fortunate. I had a bike and was given free rail passes to go anywhere in the United Kingdom. I was keen to see as much of England, Wales and Scotland as I could."

Each leave Naylor would visit new areas. He met some hospitable people through an organisation in England that arranged for local families throughout the country to host service people when they were on leave.

Naylor's friendship with Ida Penny continued to grow, and he visited her in Millom when he could. Towards the end of the war he bought a 'baby' Austin car at the airbase, which he would drive to see her.

"If a British airman was killed or failed to return, all his effects were sent home to his family. However if the airman was from the Commonwealth, his belongings were auctioned off with the proceeds sent home. I bought the Austin car for £8, which had belonged to someone from the Commonwealth who didn't come back."

Ida and Naylor.

Naylor's crew flew seven war operations to France and Belgium in August and September 1944. In October they started flying into Scandinavia, including two operations to Denmark where low flying was easier due to its flat terrain.

The following month they flew to Norway for the first time, where the operations would prove some of their most challenging and exhausting of the war. Return flights took an average of seven to nine hours, requiring the intense concentration of all of the crew, particularly Naylor. They often wouldn't return from those operations until three or four o'clock in the morning.

"We had to leave late in the afternoon and fly over the North Sea before dark. Pinpoint navigation was required to find the dropping zones, which were usually in a valley or somewhere like that."

During one of these missions Naylor's precise observational and navigational skills avoided certain catastrophe for his crew.

They were flying behind another plane from the squadron to drop people into Norway, when there was a sudden wind change. Naylor managed to access the last of the English radar and believed the planes were going off course. As the planes reached landfall in Norway, Naylor's unease continued to grow. The skipper, Doug Banbury had been told to follow the other plane, which was being directed by its own navigator. Naylor told Doug he thought they were in the wrong place, and given the great trust he had in Naylor's skills and instincts, the skipper heeded his advice to fly further along the coast until their exact location could be determined.

Within seconds of realigning the aircraft, the plane they had been following was shot down by enemy fire after flying directly over an enemy fighter station. Naylor's crew watched the tragedy unfold, realising just how close they had come to meeting the same fate.

Most of the operations into Denmark and Norway were completed successfully with just a few hampered by bad weather, or being unable to identify the drop zone or locate the reception committee on the ground.

On 15 January 1945, Naylor was promoted to Warrant Officer. The following month on the second-to-last mission made by 138 Squadron from Tempsford, Naylor's aircraft was hit by ground fire, but managed to make it safely back to base. The next day, on 22 February 1945, the crew completed its final SOE operation to Norway.

At the end of February 1945, 138 Squadron Special Operations Executive finished its special duties at Tempsford, and was transferred to Bomber Command at Tuddenham, where Naylor's crew was switched to a Lancaster bomber.

During the final days of the war in April and May 1945, every available Lancaster was used to carry out humanitarian food drops to feed desperate Dutch people in the grip of famine in the German-occupied Netherlands, where thousands had already died of starvation.

The missions were part of Operation Manna, named after the biblical miracle of God dropping bread from heaven to the starving Israelites. The low flying expertise of Naylor's crew proved advantageous, as the big bombers, which had dropped bombs from around 6000 metres, were being used to drop precious food cargo without parachutes, from as low as 120 to 150 metres.

The RAF made 3100 flights as part of Operation Manna, dropping more than 6000 tons of food. Naylor's crew flew four of these missions, one to Rotterdam on 30 April 1945, and three into The

Hague in early May. Their final operation was carried out in hazy weather, with the 16 aircraft involved accurately dropping 67 packs, carrying 74,400 pounds of food.

"These were incredibly satisfying missions. We could see the Dutch people waiting at the dropping zones and waving wildly," said Naylor.

In an amazing coincidence, many years later, Naylor met a woman back in his home town of Christchurch, New Zealand who may have been one of the people in Rotterdam waving to his plane.

Naylor and his family were at a church picnic, when his son David started chatting to a Dutch woman, named Annie Koetsdyk. When Annie mentioned she had lived in Rotterdam during the war and remembered the big Lancasters flying over delivering food, David suggested she meet Naylor, given he had flown there as part of Operation Manna.

When they compared dates and the area Naylor had flown to, it was highly likely Annie had been a recipient of the food drop from his crew.

In March 1990, Annie wrote a letter to Naylor, saying, 'To Naylor Hillary and all the other airmen, a big thank you with a hug from Annie Koetsdyk and all the other Dutchies. This is to let you know how you played a part in my life in the war. May we never forget.'

Attached to the letter was a short memoir, written by Annie, detailing her harrowing experiences during the war. She had lived in the west of Rotterdam near the harbour where most of the Germans were housed.

When the Hongerwinter (Hunger Winter) of 1944–45 hit, Annie was alone with her young baby Arie, who was almost a year old. Her first husband Arie Ryntalder had already died in a prisoner-of-war camp on Alderney in the Channel Islands at the age of 23. He was said to have escaped from other POW camps in the Netherlands and Germany after his original arrest for ignoring German instructions about labour camp registration.

Annie wrote:

"We were more than four years in the war. Most of our men were gone. They were in Germany in forced labour camps, or killed, or they worked in the Underground. The situation was bad. The Germans took more and more food away from us. I was living close to a railway station. There you could see the trains loaded with our food, but they had posters on them that translated to 'Gifts of love from the Dutch'. Don't believe that. It was our food and they took it from us. All we had were coupons, and plenty of them, for the shops, but the shops were practically empty. As time went on it got worse. We started eating sugar beets, tulip bulbs and some sorts of weeds. How bad the times were. My parents were living on the outskirts of Rotterdam. One day a German soldier came and asked Mum how many rooms she had and he wanted to see the house. He told her she could have two soldiers in and she had to do the cooking for them. They brought food and ordered poor Mum, who was as thin as a stick, to cook it. When she set the table and a plate for herself and for Dad, they laughed and took the plates away. They ate the lot while my parents were starving.

To top it off, they used the washbasin in the bedroom as a toilet and Mum had to clean it up. How do you forgive things like that? My father secretly grew potatoes and vegetables. But the Germans made him dig them up and took the vegetables with them.

There were funny times too. One Sunday morning to my horror I saw parachutes coming down. Paratroopers were over Rotterdam, in the middle of town. The Germans were shooting like mad then a bomb dropped very close by. The house was shaking and the baby cried. But when I looked outside, I had to laugh, for the bomb had dropped right on top of a train with the posters of 'gifts of love' and the train had just about disappeared. And what was in it? Coffee beans. The train must have been full for there were beans everywhere and people went outside to pick them up. And the parachutists? They were dummies. Just rubber dolls. We had a good laugh but of course the Germans were furious. How we liked things like that. In all the misery the Dutch did not lose their humour."

On her little boy's first birthday, there was nothing to eat, which Annie said was a 'very, very sad day'.

"There is nothing so bad than to hold a baby in your arms and it is crying from hunger and you have nothing to give it. How do you explain that to a little one? You pray and pray and you get a feeling you are talking to a nothing, to a deep emptiness. I felt terribly lonely. I was not able to go to family as there were no trains, trams or buses. There was no food, light, or heat, and it was bitterly cold. My legs were swollen from malnutrition. All I wanted was that it would be over. It was night. I got up and opened the curtains, which was not allowed. The Moffen would be furious. They would shoot us or plant a bomb on the house. All right with me. My faith was nil. Who can love a God who let us suffer so much? What did a little baby do to deserve this? But even though I forgot Him, He did not forget me. For a short time later, the bell rang. Funny, I thought, the Moffen would not ring the bell politely but smash the door in. I opened the door and there was the neighbour from across the road. 'What the heck are you thinking? You can see the light at the end of the street. Are you crazy?' she said. She went to the windows and closed the curtains properly. I cried and told her everything. That I felt ill, that we did not have food for two days, and the ever- crying baby was getting on my nerves.

She said, 'I am going home, but leave the door open. I will be back.' And back she came, with four sandwiches for me, and a plate of warm baby food for my boy. When I asked her where she had got it from, she said 'you had better not know'. I was so happy and grateful. My boy had a full tummy for the first time in days."

The neighbour told Annie that she and her father were taking a little handcart to the Moerdijk Bridge, where they knew a farmer who was going to give them some potatoes. There had been a lot of shooting in the area, but the neighbour said she believed they had found a way around it. The dangerous trip would take two days. She told Annie to watch for them on the second evening, and she would wave if they had some potatoes to give her.

"I waited and prayed. Again it was two foodless days. Only a

packet of cornflour from the church but my boy did not like it without milk or sugar. I got a bit of sugarbeet, which was too small to cook but he could suck at it. Then evening came and between the curtains I saw the neighbours coming. They walked very slowly and must have been very tired. They did not forget because soon she was waving. I went over in my socks and handed her my bucket. She put something in it and I went home again. It was very dark and I could not see what was in it. I felt with my hand, and then, disappointment. It was sugarbeets, as they were too big for spuds. Then morning came. I went to the bucket and what I saw in there was a dream. It was not sugarbeets, but potatoes in the bucket with swedes on the top. The tears were running down my face. We had real proper food. I knelt down and thanked the Lord for that food. There was no meat, or gravy, or butter, but who cared. My boy just loved it and kept asking for more. Then for the first time in days he fell asleep with a full tummy and rosy cheeks."

This small good fortune happened when things were at their worst in the Netherlands. Millions of people were suffering from malnutrition. People were dying every day. Although the liberation of the Netherlands was imminent, the Germans continued to retaliate against the Dutch people for acts of resistance. Annie heard on the radio that Allied forces were planning to drop food, but she didn't think the Germans would allow it to happen.

"I thought the Moffen would shoot the planes or take the food. But talks happened. The war was coming to an end and the Germans knew they had lost. The Germans were told if they touched the food or shot at the planes they would be treated as war criminals when the war was over. That would mean the death penalty so they agreed. In the meantime the British and Americans had been trained in low flying, for if they did not fly low all the food that was packed in tins and sacks would burst and the food wasted. All those years the airmen had been bombing and destroying and now there was a chance to save. Then came the big day – Manna! Food from heaven! And there came the planes, big heavy Lancasters. They flew so low we could easily see the pilots. They came by the hundreds. The people went crazy. They were

on the roofs, in trees, on top of the trains. They waved with sheets, towels, orange duster flags, waving, waving, waving! I held my boy up to the pilot. Would he have seen it? I am sure he did. Many were crying. Grown men cried openly. Nobody had seen anything like it, and down it came. On sports greens, airfields, everywhere. Tins with biscuits were the first things. Big dry biscuits especially made for us with added vitamins that were easy to digest. If they had given us fatty food first many more people would have died. Later on there was meat, flour, butter, chocolate, egg powder. So much. Hundreds and hundreds of planes came for nine days, day and night. The noise was deafening. They also dropped a million food rations for us. It still took a week before we got the food, for everything was packed in tins and bags, and had to be distributed. Then a man came into the street and announced we could get one kilo of biscuits per person with one coupon. We went with a pillowslip to put the biscuits in, and also got milk powder. How well it was organised.

It must have been marvellous for the airmen to do such a job. When the food droppings came to an end they were allowed to have their own fun. They made little parachutes from hankies, packed with a note and things like chocolate, a bar of soap, or a toy. There was even a little doll for a Dutch girl from an American airman. The notes had wishes of strength, 'keep the chin up', 'not long now', 'we are coming', things like that. On the roofs of the houses people painted messages, like 'thank you boys' or 'thank you Tommies and Yanks'."

On 5 May 1945 the whole of the Netherlands was finally free.

"Finally after five years the time we had been waiting for had come. We were free. The Moffen were going home. Some, I felt sorry for, as they had a family and kids. What would they find when they got home? Gone was all the bravery, the big strong soldiers with their heavy boots who came into our country singing. Skinny and down they went, with worn out uniforms.

The lights would go on again all over the world. There would be work again. The towns would be built up again. There would be clothes and food. And there would be a future again for us and our children. We knew that God had led us through this terrible time. It was hard sometimes not to despair. He did not promise us an easy journey but we had a safe homecoming."

After the war, Annie struggled to bring little Arie up on her own as a widow, with no assistance from the government. She got a job in a children's home and managed to get by. Then the War Graves Commission asked if she would like to tend the grave of one of the fallen from the Allied forces, which only had a little wooden cross. The dead airman had been shot down over Rotterdam. His name was Harry Clothier, and he had come from Kaiapoi, about 20 minutes north of Christchurch, New Zealand. Annie took a photograph of little Arie placing flowers on the grave and sent it to Harry's heartbroken mother in New Zealand. This started a very special correspondence between the two women, with Annie later referring to Mrs Clothier as 'Mother Lucie', saying she was 'so sweet and caring'.

After writing for 14 years, Annie decided to immigrate to New Zealand, believing she could offer Arie a better life there than she could in Holland. She settled in Christchurch in 1960 at the age of 42 and found it difficult at first to learn English, and take on unfamiliar jobs. Tragically, Annie lost her son Arie at the age of 23, following an illness. He was the same age as his father at his death, and incredibly they died on the same day – 31 October.

Annie remarried, and she and second husband Gerard Koetsdyk ran an arts and crafts boutique in Riccarton Road called The Navajo, which specialised in pottery by well-known New Zealand artists. Gerard died in 1985.

In a newspaper article in 1993, Annie remembered the meeting with Naylor at a church picnic during the 1960s, when a young boy heard her accent and asked her about the war.

"I told him that I lived in western Rotterdam, where it was really bad. In answer to the other question I told him we were very hungry and had been saved by the Allied food drops. He told me there was somebody I should meet. He took me to his father, Naylor G Hillary, one of the food droppers. It was just so unbelievable. I had met one of

our lifesavers. I thanked him. We talked and we laughed. Then I gave him a big hug. He had saved my life and those of hundreds of other people."

The following Sunday, Naylor took a wartime diary to church to show Annie. It confirmed the drop he had made in Rotterdam during Operation Manna was very close to where she had been living.

"So really, it was very likely that I did wave to him that day."

Annie returned to the Netherlands to visit but made New Zealand her home. She died in 1997 at the age of 78.

O n 8 May, following Operation Manna, 138 Squadron was transferred to Operation Exodus, which brought Allied prisoners-of-war back to the United Kingdom. During these operations in May and June 1945, 443 Avro Lancasters plus many other aircraft brought home over 15,000 repatriated POWs from all over Europe. A day after their transfer, Naylor's crew flew one of eight aircraft which brought home 195 British POWs from Juvincourt, France.

Naylor flew several other missions as part of Operation Exodus, including 'Operation Cooks' Tour' on 31 May 1945, which took 10 passengers on an aerial tour of the Rhur. In June, he was on the first of two low flying missions over Germany as part of Operation Baedeker, to allow ground crews and administration staff to monitor bomb damage.

The following month, Naylor's crew started photographic survey work across Northern Europe as part of Operation Revue to update the region's mapping. They took aerial photographs of numerous cities, ports, railway stations, rivers, road and rail bridges and other infrastructure in Germany, Norway, France, Spain and Holland.

During one flight to France, Naylor's skipper, Doug Banbury, who had been promoted to Flight Lieutenant at the end of the war, decided to have a bit of fun on the way back to Tuddenham, flying straight up the Champs Élysées in Paris.

"We got in a bit of trouble for that and were severely repri-
manded when we got back to base," said Naylor.

An entry in the Tuddenham ORB (Operational Record Book)
from 15 August 1945 highlights the joy felt on the base when hostilities in the Far East also ceased, and war was officially at an end: "Following on the official declaration of the cessation of hostilities in the
Far East, work in the Squadron was limited to a minimum, and after
an early 'Stand Down', all personnel were invited to join in numerous
celebrations organised on the station. This they did in no uncertain
manner."

Soon after, on 28 August, Naylor was promoted to Flying Officer,
and just a few days later, his crew was transferred to Værnes, Norway
for the final couple of weeks of their service. He kept a railway ticket
from this period, to a Norwegian destination called Hell, a name that
could easily have been applied to some of the devastated cities in
Europe by the end of the war.

Naylor's crew in barracks in Norway.

After completing their final two missions under Operation Revue, Naylor's crew returned to Tuddenham on 18 September. This would be their final flight together as a crew. These brave young men, most of whom were aged only in their twenties, had displayed such incredible courage during their top secret war operations.

Naylor never saw Doug Banbury again, but he kept in touch with engineer, Johnny Harland for a while until Johnny went to South Africa and they eventually lost touch. Back in New Zealand, Naylor was best man at air bomber, Ray Jorgenson's wedding to his wife Joyce.

As a man of the church, Naylor said his work during his time at Tempsford, although highly dangerous, sat well with him.

"It felt like we were doing something good at Tempsford. It would not have been easy to keep one's faith while at the same time dropping bombs. In England I spent time praying in little chapels there. I believe it helped sustain me in those terrible times."

Naylor set sail on a troop ship bound for New Zealand almost immediately after his last operation with 138 Squadron, and during the journey, had plenty of time to finish modifying and polishing a model aeroplane of a Stirling Mark III, which he had purchased as a rough brass casting while stationed at Wratton Common.

"The ground crew there produced them. I don't know where they got the brass. It was quite a good model, although I knew it would require a tremendous amount of filing to get it to the polished stage. After I bought it, I put it in my kitbag and thought I might do something with it someday."

After Naylor was posted to 138 Squadron he decided to try to convert the model from the Stirling Mark III (used extensively for bombing over Europe) to the lightened Stirling Mark IV, which his crew had flown at Tempsford.

"I wouldn't like to think how many hours I spent filing the mid upper gun turret and the nose turret off the model to make it look more like a Stirling Mark IV. I didn't finish it until I was on the boat

Naylor's modified model of the Stirling Mark IV.

on the way back from England, when I had plenty of time to get it polished and looking quite good. After I got home, I had the plane mounted, and it meant so much to me over the years."

Naylor arrived back in New Zealand on 21 December 1945 and was demobilised on 28 February 1946. After his return, he continued to write to Ida Penny.

They stopped corresponding for a while when Ida was ill and spent some time in hospital at Whitehaven, but resumed writing when she was better. The couple decided to become engaged, and Ida went out to New Zealand.

They were married in 1948, at Durham Street Methodist Church, in Christchurch, where they settled, and later had their children, Pamela and David.

After the war, Naylor went back to work at his father's real estate business, Hillary and Baxter which he eventually took over. He became one of the city's senior urban valuers, and eventually did more valuing work than selling houses. Naylor worked there until his retirement when he was 72. In later years the company became Hillary and Marshall.

He and Ida made several trips back to the United Kingdom and visited Tempsford together, which had changed significantly since the war years. In 1953, Tempsford effectively became a village of two halves after the A1 highway was built right through the centre of it.

Most of the airfield runways were ripped up for hard fill for the roads. Although Naylor took Ida to Tempsford, he never told her the full story about his wartime exploits.

"Ida knew I had flown from there but not where I had been or what I'd been doing. The whole thing was so tied up in secrecy that we couldn't discuss things, but she understood."

Naylor remained a committed churchman, and was devoted to the Methodist church throughout his life.

Naylor and Ida at Diamond Harbour, Christchurch, New Zealand.

Until he was aged in his mid-nineties, he was a trustee of the Hyman Marks Trust, which was established in 1895 in Christchurch to provide charitable grants to people in need.

Naylor's wife Ida passed away in 2014, and he continued to live in their home until the last few weeks of his life, when he went into care. He passed away in September 2017 at the age of 102, a man who was much loved and respected by his children, five grandchildren and four great-grandchildren.

During his service, Naylor received a number of medals, including the 1939-45 Star with Bomber Command Clasp, France and Germany Star, Defence Medal, War Medal, and New Zealand War Service Medal, He was delighted to receive the Légion d'Honnéur medal from the President of the French Republic in 2016, when details of his top secret service came to light. It was a fitting final tribute.

Naylor receiving the Légion d'Honnéur medal from the Honorary French Consul in Christchurch, Martine Marshall-Durieux, in 2016.

Following Naylor's passing, his daughter, Pam and her husband David Bissland, donated Naylor's French Légion d'Honnéur medal to his former secondary school, St Andrew's College, in Christchurch. Given Naylor's devotion to the church, it was fitting the College put the medal on display in its new Centennial Chapel. This impressive structure replaced the College's old Memorial Chapel, which was constructed after the war to commemorate the Old Collegians and staff who made the ultimate sacrifice. The Memorial Chapel was damaged beyond repair during the Christchurch earthquakes of 2010 and 2011.

Naylor was a highly respected Old Collegian at St Andrew's throughout his life, and the College meant a lot to him. He was a special guest at the College's Centenary celebrations in March 2017, when he cut the Centenary birthday cake with his great-grandson, Henry Bissland, who was a Year 2 student at the time. Naylor's son

David, and three grandsons, Gareth, Rhys and James Bissland also attended St Andrew's.

Incredibly, Naylor was almost 102 years old at the special Centenary celebrations, older than the College itself.

Pam and David never imagined when they asked for some photographs for Naylor's 100th birthday display, that their request would lead to such interesting revelations about his life. After finding out about Naylor's involvement in 138 Squadron at Tempsford, David became passionate about researching its history.

Naylor and his great-grandson, Henry Bissland, in March 2017, at the St Andrew's College Centenary celebrations. *Photograph taken by Clinton Lloyd and courtesy of St Andrew's College.*

During a visit to the United Kingdom, the couple were given a personal tour of Gibraltar Farm by Lady Erroll, who showed them what was left of the airfield, and the famous Gibraltar Farm Barn, where the agents were kitted out before being spirited away on their secret missions by the Tempsford squadrons.

"We drove down what had been the old runways, and arrived at the barn. As we approached the entrance we thought about Naylor, his crew, and all who had left through those doors to fight for their own and our freedom, never to return. A shrine inside the barn immortalised many of those brave souls, while in the fields outside, several trees had plaques at their base in memory of those lost," said David.

Over 80 aircraft were lost from Tempsford, with 623 airmen from the 138 and 161 Squadrons killed including 31 Australians, 16 New Zealanders, 58 Polish, and 78 Canadians.

It is believed 995 agents were dropped into occupied Europe by parachute from the base, with 485 landed by aircraft. A further 575 agents, VIPs and shot-down RAF aircrew were brought back to the UK.

The squadrons dropped 29,000 containers and 10,000 packages into enemy occupied territory during their years of operation, and were said to have 'liberated' countless cases of cognac, champagne and premier wines.

In 2013, His Royal Highness, Prince Charles unveiled a memorial at Tempsford to commemorate the 75 female agents who left from Tempsford, of whom 29 were arrested, 16 executed, three died of illnesses while imprisoned, and one committed suicide using a cyanide L pill before being captured.

The memorial doesn't mention the hundreds of male agents who also left from Tempsford, many of whom made the ultimate sacrifice. Each year during summer, remaining veterans, and relatives of veterans gather at Gibraltar Farm barn, courtesy of Lady Erroll, to remember and honour their colleagues and family members. The Bisslands returned to Tempsford again in 2017 for the TVARA gathering, meeting other relatives of the 138 and 161 Squadron crews.

"The number of family members attending the Tempsford gathering grows each year. It is an honour to represent our veterans, recognise their bravery, and celebrate the vital role they played in the war effort."

I t seems incredible that the wartime work of the hundreds of men and women based at Tempsford Airfield remained one of the biggest secrets of the war for years. Details finally started to emerge after 1972, when operations at Tempsford came off the Official Secrets List and information became freely available in the National Archives at Kew.

Although the local people in the villages of Tempsford and

Everton regularly saw the RAF crews, they had no idea about the sort of clandestine activities they were engaged in. Night after night they watched the aircraft go out and may have heard them return in the early hours of the morning. However they never realised the men and women in civilian clothes being driven from a manor house in the village, up the road which said 'closed to the public' to Tempsford Airfield, were among the most famous agents of World War II, embarking on some of the most dangerous missions of the war.

The courage shown by the agents, and the crews, like Naylor's in the 138 and 161 Squadrons cannot be underestimated, with their remarkable efforts and bravery assisting the Allied forces to victory.

At the time their work was top secret, but it is now remembered, honoured, and will be never forgotten.

4

THE WĘGRZYN FAMILY

ON THE EVE of World War II, Józef Węgrzyn and his wife Aniela were like many couples living a peaceful, happy life with their family in the Second Polish Republic, which had been established in 1918 at the end of World War I.

However within a couple of weeks in September 1939, their idyllic rural lifestyle was shattered, when Poland was invaded from the west by Nazi Germany and the east by Soviet Russia.

Poland's independent status was destroyed, with millions of Polish people later persecuted, murdered or interned.

The Węgrzyn family lived in the small Polish settlers' colony of Ostrów, in southeast Poland. This was among several colonies set up near the town of Ostrów at the end of World War I, in a region formerly part of the Ukraine.

The couple's large extended families had settled in Ostrów in the early 1920s, where there was plenty of land available for them to farm and raise their children.

Józef was a builder and a farmer, while Aniela also did a lot of farm work to help support their children. Their eldest daughter, Maria was born in 1925, followed by sister Józefa in 1927, brother Janek in 1929, sister Władysława (Władzia) in 1931, sister Franciszka (Frania) in 1935, and little brother Bronislaw (Bronek), born in 1938, who was just one year old when war was declared on 1 September 1939.

The family loved their simple, rural lifestyle, with grandparents, aunties, uncles and cousins on both sides living close by.

Aniela and Józef Węgrzyn with family on their wedding day in Poland in 1923.

Both Maria and Józefa, the two eldest children, remembered their pre-war childhood with great affection.

"It was fun to be a part of a big family and we enjoyed freedom in the nice open spaces. We had a large forest nearby, with high majestic trees and other trees with fruit and nuts. We used to play there, and pick mushrooms, strawberries and blueberries. On one side of the forest grew highly scented flowers such as violets, lilies, dahlias and many others. We used to run wild in the high grass, picking flowers and taking them home to Mum. I loved the pine forest with its masses of pine cones, which we gathered into sacks for the fire. The pine needles felt like a carpet under our feet, with the magnificent broad branches of the trees creating semi-darkness," they said.

"In the summer, during long school holidays, we helped with the harvest of wheat, oats, and barley, and in the autumn, potatoes. Some years, swarms of locusts would fly over the wheat crops, and eventually destroy them. We would run around killing the locusts with tree branches, or pack them into bottles and kill them later with boiling water.

"We also had free time for sports, like netball and other childhood games, and our cousins, Maria and Franek Skałka, who lived nearby, sometimes joined us. They were our playmates, and we walked to school and church together. People in Ostrów were very religious and we attended Mass, Benediction and Devotions in summer and winter.

"At school we were taught embroidery, knitting and sewing in senior classes by a teacher who was quite demanding. We made our own fun and were lucky to have our grandparents, aunties and uncles living near us. We enjoyed visiting them frequently, and playing in their large interesting gardens, full of fruit trees and flowers.

"Aunty Zosia and Uncle Aleksander were very friendly and cheerful. They let us climb their high cherry trees and pick and eat the cherries to our heart's delight. Aunty Zosia was an accomplished seamstress and sometimes helped our mother to make dresses for us. Another uncle owned a farm 8km away, next to a large village, where we children would also help to harvest potatoes and other vegetables.

"The winters were long and cold, with hard frosts. We loved the snow, although we often felt very cold when we walked the 2.5km home from school. Sometimes our father drove us in the horse and cart, or if the snow was very deep, he would take us to school on a horse-drawn sledge. After school, we would make snowmen, or slide on the soles of our shoes on the frozen river near the school. We would give each other rides on sledges made by our father. Our happy life ended when World War II broke out."

Soon after, the family was deported to a labour camp in Siberia, where they were told they would stay prisoners for life.

O n the third day of the war, German planes bombed the Węgrzyn's village of Ostrów, along with surrounding towns and villages.

"We heard the screams and wailing of wounded and shocked people. The Germans were shooting without mercy. Many Polish people died in battle in our locality. But a greater number of Jewish people perished. The German soldiers ransacked their shops and strew their merchandise in the marketplace, which was already crowded with the wounded and the dead. In the nearby town of Krystynopol there stood abandoned, empty buildings. All Polish hearts were filled with grief and sadness," said Józefa.

In the meantime, Ukrainian settlers declared a ruthless vengeance on the Polish colonists, declaring a 'free Ukraine must rise again'. They stole whatever they could from the Polish people, killing any who dared to complain.

Many of the men in the Węgrzyn's colony were quickly drafted into the Polish Army, leaving mothers and children bereft of sons, husbands and fathers. With the Polish Army directed to the west to repel the German invasion, the eastern border was poorly guarded, leaving the way almost clear for the Soviets to invade Poland on 17 September 1939. Just a small contingent of Polish soldiers bravely fought until their defeat.

A few days later, the Russian Army reached the town of Sokal, close to Ostrów. Together with Nazi Germany, they imposed a new border on Poland, with the western side guarded by the German forces and the lands east of the rivers Pisa, Narew, Bug and San, guarded by Russian soldiers. Only a few Poles dared to attempt crossing the border, as most who did were either shot or deported to Russia.

Poland was now roughly divided in half, with both the German and Soviet regimes hostile to the Second Polish Republic and its people.

At the start of the invasion, the Soviet Union ceased to recognise the Polish state, and because the Russian authorities regarded pre-war service to Poland as a 'crime against revolution' started to arrest, imprison and massacre Polish military personnel and civilians. Tens of thousands of prisoners-of-war were also killed, with the mass deportation of 1.2 million Poles later carried out in four waves during 1940 and 1941.

The Red Army also confiscated and redistributed private and state-owned Polish property. Ethnic tensions were exploited, with other ethnic groups encouraged by the Russians to incite violence against the Poles.

The occupation of Poland by Nazi Germany was equally cruel and devastating, with terrible atrocities committed against the Polish people, including the furious bombardment of Warsaw at the start of the war.

Following its invasion, Nazi Germany sent most of Poland's 3.5 million Jews into newly established ghettos. When this system proved unsustainable, the Germans outlined plans for the total genocide of the Jews in extermination camps. They set up a number of concentration camps in Poland, including one of the largest, and most infamous, Auschwitz.

With a reign of terror having descended on its country, the Polish government was forced to operate in exile from London.

Ostrów ended up on the German side of the new border, which meant the Węgrzyn family was unable to visit the town to do their shopping or attend their local Roman Catholic parish church. They had to go eastwards, to the nearby village of

Gluchow, where there were few provisions available, apart from salt, kerosene and cotton.

The Russians forced many local people into work such as repairing roads or felling forests.

"Every day they would come up with new schemes. They held lengthy committee meetings for days, planning when to deport the Polish population into Russia, and deciding who to deprive of their cattle, horses and wheat," said Józefa.

On 10 February 1940, on a bitterly cold morning before dawn, the family awoke to the sound of banging and somebody shouting loudly in Russian, 'Open the door'.

Aniela Węgrzyn opened the door to be met by around ten Russian soldiers, some who came into the house, and some who stood by the door. The ones inside the house ordered the family to dress and then sit on the cold earthen floor while they ransacked their home in search of guns. Aniela told the soldiers they would need bread if they were being taken away, but a soldier said they would not need it, as they would be provided with food when they got to their destination in another Polish province. The family was hurried onto horse and carts with the few possessions and provisions they could muster, and were soon passing through the settlement. They could hear shouts, crying, painful moaning, cows lowing in their stables, and dogs whining at the sight of their owners leaving home. When all the residents of the settlement were loaded onto the carts, they departed, one after the other. Sorrow overwhelmed them all, as they left their homes, possessions and their old lives behind forever.

Second eldest daughter, Józefa had stayed the previous night with her Babcia (grandmother), Franciszka Majda, Aniela's mother, who had been widowed in 1934. She awoke to the sound of a Russian soldier shouting at her to get up and get dressed.

"I immediately got up and saw Grandma with my aunty and uncle and their children sitting on the floor by a window. They said 'Get dressed and come here, we have something to tell you'. The room soon filled with Russian soldiers who began tipping clothing on to the floor out of wardrobes and wooden chests. Some guarded the house, the stables and the doorways so we couldn't escape. After they ransacked the house they told us to get out and board the carts, but forbade us to eat. We were driven away to Gluchow."

It was snowing and the family was only lightly dressed. Józefa was anxious to be reunited with her parents and brothers and sisters. Once they arrived at the village, they were told to leave their belongings and go into an old schoolroom. Józefa rejoined her mother and family, and their names were checked off on a list.

After a couple of hours they were told to board the carts again, which had been emptied of many of their belongings by some Ukrainian locals.

Aniela wrapped a quilt around her three youngest children Władzia, Frania and Bronek, while Maria, Janek and Józefa sat on a wooden seat in the cart. The temperature continued to fall, and by the time they completed the 8km journey to the train station at Parhacz, the horses were exhausted, and the family's hands and legs were frozen.

On their arrival, they were told to immediately board some train cattle wagons, which were soon overcrowded, with up to 30 or 40 people assigned to each. The wagons were incredibly cold inside. There was little space for the family's belongings, and no room for them to lie down and sleep. The train stood stationary all day, and was guarded by the Russians, who wouldn't allow anyone to exit, or even look outside the tiny high windows, which were secured with steel bars.

At midnight the train finally left the station, with many people crying in despair, and some fainting in the terrible conditions. Although the Russian soldiers told the Poles they were being taken to another Polish province, they knew this wasn't the truth, and they were headed for forced labour camps in Siberia.

Maria Węgrzyn said as the train began to move, there was a terrible grinding noise from the steel wagon wheels, accompanied by the loud banging of the carriage couplings.

"The children and many people began to cry. Some pushed their faces against the iron-grilled openings above the upper shelves to catch their last glimpse of Poland. Our mother and Aunty Zosia began to sing the well-known Marian hymn, *Nie płacz juz dziecino*, 'Don't cry my little child, though you are in pain. Just huddle under the mantle of Mary your Mother. She will heal all your wounds. Cease crying, dear child, cease crying. Don't cry, don't cry, because your heavenly Mother has always a caring heart for all her children.' The hymn had a sad melody, and every time I heard it sung at Polish religious celebrations, I was back in that wagon."

The train rattled on at speed by day, and at night would stop in the isolated open countryside, so no one could approach the train to help the people or give them food or water.

"People would bang loudly on the big sliding side doors of the wagons, begging for water from the Russian guards outside, who would shout back to silence the voices. Whenever they did open the sliding doors we would give them our small buckets, which they would fill with dirty snow. When the snow thawed, we would have barely two cups full of water, mixed with dirt and soot. We were not allowed out to go to the toilet, and had to go in a hole in the floor of each wagon, with no privacy." said Maria.

When the train reached Ostróg, the family was transferred to a Russian train, and soon after the journey recommenced, they could see the Russian border, lined with posts topped with barbed wire.

A few hours later, they arrived at a main station, where the wagon doors were opened.

The Russian soldiers told the Polish people to get out and gave them some soup and bread, the first meal they had eaten since leaving their home.

"The soup cost a ruble, and was thin and watery. It consisted of about three pieces of meat floating in a bucket with a small amount of stale rice. Some people ate it but others threw it out. We were allotted a ration of 200 grams of bread per person. None of this food tasted good. We were lucky we still had some of the provisions we had brought with us from Poland. The water rations were dire as no water was available at the station. We were all thirsty, especially the children. We sucked the icicles snapped off the window bars, and continued to drink the muddied snow collected by the rail tracks," said Józefa.

This routine continued at further stations along the route. The price of soup and stale bread went up at each stop, although the quality of the food never improved.

The difficult journey continued, with the family enduring extreme cold, hunger and thirst.

After two gruelling weeks, they arrived in a large town in the Sverdlovsk Oblast in the Ural Mountains, where the family learned the people from their wagon were being sent to a Siberian communist work settlement named Czary, another 40km away.

The journey was miserable. The family travelled in an unreliable bus, which broke down constantly. They had to wait in minus 40 degree temperatures while the driver and his assistant carried out repairs.

It was dark by the time they arrived at Czary, and the family was exhausted and frozen. The Russian authorities directed them to a large school, where they were told to bunk down for the night. All their belongings were stacked outside, with guards at the doorway not allowing them to exit.

"We were so tired we immediately lay down to rest and sleep but had barely dozed off when we could feel we were being bitten. On checking, we found an infestation of lice. The walls were covered with crawling red bugs. We didn't sleep all night and rose in the morning to find our bodies covered in welts the size of our fingers. Then we went outside to discover half of our belongings were missing. They had been stolen by the Russians."

By day, the family was able to see their new home. Czary had houses lining either side of a main street. There was just one shop in the middle of the settlement, from which they would be given their daily bread ration, 300 grams per working adult, and 200 grams per child. There was also a supervisor's office, a small prison, a bakery, and a hospital, known as the 'death house' by those in the settlement, as most people who went in seemed to be quickly dispatched to the local cemetery.

The family was told to inspect the living quarters they had been allotted with Aniela's mother, Franciszka Majda, her brother Pawel Majda, his wife Maria, and their two daughters. The small, filthy loghouse was crawling with lice, bugs and vermin, which would fall from the walls and ceilings on to the families at night.

Apart from a potbelly stove, the house was completely bare, with no furniture to sit or lie down on. The Russians brought the family some wood and told them they could light the stove, but with the wood frozen and damp, and the chimney blocked with a thick layer of soot, the room quickly filled with smoke.

Once they managed to get the fire burning cleanly, Aniela put a pot of water on the stove, added some beans, and that was the family's first dinner at Czary.

Józef Węgrzyn and his eldest son Janek did their best to create a homelier environment, said Józefa.

"Tata and Janek felled a pine tree in the forest and eventually made a rough table, beds, and a cupboard to store dishes, pots and pans, which at the time we also lacked. They even carved wooden spoons and made racks for storage. This was our total inventory of furniture."

Within a day or two of their arrival, the local Russian commandant decreed that all people aged between 15 and 60 years old had to work in the massive pine forests nearby, which stretched for thousands of hectares.

The harsh reality of their new life as forced labourers in Siberia quickly hit home. Polish people were assigned to many different tasks, such as felling trees, hand sawing the large logs, and uprooting tree stumps.

The women were made to burn the smaller branches, shovel snow, carry bricks, and help to build houses.

Polish deportees cutting timber in a Serbian labour
camp in 1940.

Throughout the brutal winter months, the thousands of pine trees in the forest had to be debarked to a certain height with the branches trimmed. Then a 'Y' shaped groove would be cut into the trees, with a crampon affixed at the bottom of the groove. A small clay dish was attached to the crampon, ready to catch the resin that would weep from the pine trees in spring. It was incredibly arduous work, made even more difficult by the freezing conditions.

All workers at Czary were woken at 4am and had to be at their workstations by 6am. A Russian policeman would inspect the huts for cleanliness each morning, so with the adults already at work, the children had to rise early to scrub and wash the floors. If the floors were not cleaned to the policeman's liking, the children would go without their bread ration that day.

Each evening, when the workers returned, they would queue up at the store for soup and bread, sometimes for up to three hours. There were occasions when the Russian workers had eaten all of the rations, and the Poles had to pay two rubles for a bowl of watery soup with a few grains of rice and some herbs.

The harsh conditions took a terrible toll on Józef and Aniela Węgrzyn.

In Poland, just before the war, Józef had had an operation on his lower skull, which had left him unable to do the hard labour demanded by the Russians. He was given a job making barrels for storing the pine resin instead. The 'norm' or requirement was for him to make 16 barrels a day, which was an impossible task. As punishment for not achieving the 'norm', the Russian authorities took Józef's coupon book for bread rations, and reduced his daily ration to 200 grams, which he had to pay for himself. It was a dreadful blow for the family.

Aniela had to work in bitter conditions in the clay pit, mixing mud with her bare feet, in temperatures as low as minus 42 degrees. She and a Polish man named Mr Chorzepa would then mold the clay into cup-shaped dishes, and fire them in a kiln, ready to be used for collecting the pine resin. After two months she contracted tuberculosis of the lungs and was very ill, constantly vomiting blood.

Between them, the couple barely made ten rubles a month, which wasn't enough to provide extra food for themselves, let alone their six children. After a few months, Józef fell seriously ill, and it was left to Aniela and eldest daughter, Maria to support the family from the paltry amount they were paid for their forced labour.

Maria had been sent to work in the 'kalinkas' or clearings deep in the forests, several kilometres from the family's settlement. Her designated area included two hills with thousands of fully-grown pine trees. In the winter, she would carry a bag full of wooden wedges and crampons, a hammer, clay dishes, and a ladder. A young Polish man was responsible for scraping the deep gashes high in the trees, into which Maria would affix the crampons. Although they were assigned to the same part of the forest, the areas were so vast they never saw each other.

"I didn't catch sight of him once. We had to work alone anyway, as we were forbidden to meet up with any of our fellow Polish workers in the forest," she said.

When the snow was firm, the forest was relatively easy to walk in. But in spring, the ground was slippery and strewn with fallen trees and dead wood, which Maria would have to scramble over with her load. In the summer months she had the difficult task of collecting the pine resin, which had accumulated in the clay dishes attached to each tree.

Maria's daily 'norm' was to collect 63 kilograms, or around four heavy buckets full of resin, which she had to lug right to the top of the hills where the storage barrels were located. A Russian woman would come each day to check her output.

"The cups were out of reach from the ground, so I had to use a forked branch to take them down and drain them into the buckets. Sometimes a cup would tip all of the resin on to my head, covering me with a sticky mess. I had to use kerosene at the end of the day to clean myself, as there was no soap."

Hordes of vicious forest mosquitoes were a constant irritation.

"We had to wear netting over our heads, otherwise work was impossible."

Another hazard were the large wild Russian bears, which roamed the forests, attracted by the tasty pine cones, full of seeds, which had fallen to the ground.

"I'm still filled with dread and fear when I think about the loud crackling sound a bear made when it stood on dry branches on the forest floor. But at the time, I would work from pine tree to pine tree without too much concern. I would pray constantly throughout the long day to stay safe," said Maria.

Although the bears were generally not interested in humans, one large bear stalked a Polish girl from Ostrów named Maria Holun, who was petrified with fear. Eventually a Russian overseer shot the bear, which was so huge it took 12 men to carry its carcass back to the settlement.

Maria lived away from her family in small barracks in a forest glade, which had been built by one of their former neighbours from Ostrów, Franek Feliksiak. The family was deeply upset when he was killed in the forest, crushed by a falling pine tree he had just sawn.

Franek had been deported to Siberia at the same time as the

Węgrzyn family, but his wife and three children had remained behind in Ostrów. When informed of Franek's death by letter, his wife 'went into despair'. She wrote back to the Węgrzyns, with news that the Russian authorities had destroyed every home in the Ostrów colony, with all the land ploughed over into one large field.

Franek Feliksiak's wife and children were later murdered by Ukrainian guerillas. Their bodies were thrown down the family's well.

In the forest barracks there were two rooms, with six teenage boys in one, and six teenage girls in the other. A wood-burning stove stood in the middle.

Maria's good friend, Wanda Przeniczna, was one of the other girls in the barracks. She had been deported to Siberia with her aunty, who she had been visiting at the time, while her parents remained in Poland.

With no information about her parents' wellbeing and given her terrible circumstances, Wanda was constantly depressed.

"Wanda was a bit older than me, so I felt comforted in her presence. She was a big cuddly girl and used to sleep next to me and keep me warm, as I was so skinny. After we all finally left Czary, we never met up again in our lives."

Each person in the barracks was given a 500 millilitre metal mug, which was their only utensil for eating. Outside there was a well in which they could wash.

"On rising, we would boil water in our mugs, take a lump of bread, then head out to work in the dark. Fortunately, some cranberries grew in the forest at certain times of the year, which we could pick on the way."

When they got back in the evening, the young workers would be given their bread ration, usually very late at night.

"Because of the vitamin deficiency in my diet I ended up with night blindness. The Russians refused to give our bread rations to another person, so the girls in the barracks had to lead me to the roll call where the bread was distributed."

Maria (fifth from left) with some of her forest co-workers at the
Czary forced labour camp in Siberia, in 1940.

In Maria's absence, Józefa and Janek cared for their younger
brother and sisters, who, like all the younger children at Czary, were
required to go to school.

During her first year in Russia in 1940, Józefa attended a local
Russian school, in Standard 4 Primary.

"Mr Piotr Pawlowicz was our teacher, but eventually he was
arrested. Our next appointed teacher was very anti-religion and nasty
to us Polish children. The following year I did not attend school, and
to supplement our meagre rations, I would gather mushrooms and
pick berries such as blackberries, blueberries and raspberries, which
grew in the forests in the Ural Mountains."

Józefa was able to use Maria's coupon book and would sometimes
barter with a Russian woman for half a litre of milk, or even some
sweets, which were a luxury. During their two years in the camp,
lollies were only distributed twice and the children had to queue all
day to get them. Dried fish was sent to the settlement a few times a
year. Sometimes it tasted good, but often it stank with kerosene or
petrol. Sugar was only supplied a couple of times a year. There was a

regular supply of vodka and salami, but the only Poles who received this were those who had befriended the Russians, or who had fulfilled their 'norm' and were invited to eat and drink with them.

During the winter months, Maria had Sundays off work, and was able to return to Czary to see her family, including her beloved maternal grandmother, Franciszka Majda, who was in the settlement, along with several aunties and uncles.

She would also have her weekly 'bath', which was badly needed. One Sunday, on returning to Czary, Maria noticed Józefa had her arm in plaster. While waiting in the queue for bread, she had been crushed by desperate people trying to get their small ration before the supply ran out.

In the summer of 1941, Józefa would occasionally help Maria to gather the pine resin, and would stay with her in the forest barracks.

"We would work all day, returning in the evening. To forget our constant hunger, we would spend all evening in talk and laughter before retiring. Next morning before dawn, we would all walk to our workstations in a different direction. Maria and I would walk far into the forest, away from everyone. I was very scared of the bears and prayed we wouldn't encounter one. At the end of each day, I was glad to be back at the barracks."

On one occasion, the sisters were caught in one of the frequent thunderstorms over the vast forests, with forked lightning directly above them, said Maria.

"The storms were the reason there were so many fallen trees, and the forest floor was constantly wet. Józefa wept and trembled so much during one storm, I had to take her straight back to the barracks."

Death was never far away at Czary, with an ever-increasing number of Polish graves in the local cemetery. Typhoid, dysentery, and other illnesses struck down many men, women and children. Others died from hunger and severe cold.

"So many people who came from our colony of Ostrów died and were buried in the forest cemetery among the shrubbery alongside the Russian graves. Even those who were severely ill still hoped to recover and return to Poland. But tragically they died, and never had that happy moment of returning home," said Józefa.

People struggled with the arduous work, from which there was no respite, even at Christmas, Easter and Pentecost. Sick Polish people were still forced to go out to work.

In the harsh conditions their clothes and boots soon became damaged and worn out. Supplies of clothing came to Czary twice a year, but the local Russians took all the best items.

The Poles were left with the worst clothes, but most had no money to buy them anyway. Instead they made their own footwear from the bark of lime trees and clothes from sacking. For headgear they wore Russian style fur hats, made from white hare skins. This was the 'uniform' of the deportee in Siberia.

Józef Węgrzyn's health continued to deteriorate. Aniela's older sister Małgorzata Skałka was also very ill, with a severe form of tuberculosis and bowel cancer. She suffered terribly for six months with no medical care or medication, and died on 1 December 1940.

"What sorrow engulfed our whole extended family. Our aunty left four children, with her youngest son, two-year-old Ludwik, dying soon after her death, followed by the next youngest son, Wladek, two months later. Her husband Jan Skałka worked to support the remaining two children, Maria, aged 12, and Franek, who was 10 years old," said Józefa.

Other family members in the settlement included Uncle Józef Majda, his wife Jadwiga and their two sons Dominik and Józef, who both died at the settlement; and Aunty Zosia (née Majda) with her husband Aleksander Skałka and their two-year-old daughter Maria.

The family lived in dire poverty and if it wasn't for the kindness of others, particularly during the cruel winter months, many more of them would have perished.

In contrast, the Russians at Czary were well paid. They had gardens and cows, so did not fare as badly.

This gruelling routine continued until August 1941, when an unexpected turn of events saw Russia declare a one-off amnesty for Polish citizens living in the Soviet Union, resulting in a temporary stop of persecutions.

The remarkable turnaround came after Operation Barbarossa, when Nazi Germany turned on its former ally, and invaded the Soviet Union in June 1941. This led to the collapse of the German-Soviet Nonaggression Treaty of 1939.

Now at war with Nazi Germany, Soviet leader Joseph Stalin began to seek help from other countries opposing Germany.

With the encouragement of British Foreign Office diplomat, Anthony Eden, talks were started between General Władysław Sikorski, Prime Minister of the Polish government-in-exile, and Ivan Maisky, the Soviet Ambassador to London, in a bid to re-establish diplomatic relations with Poland.

This led to Sikorski visiting the Soviet Union on a diplomatic mission, and the formation of the Sikorski-Maisky Agreement between the two countries. All previous pacts with Nazi Germany were declared null and void, invalidating the partition of Poland.

Despite being in exile in London, General Sikorski was an important figurehead for the Polish people.

He continued to control the Polish armed forces, and had signed a Polish-British Military Agreement in August 1940, promising the Polish forces would fight alongside the British.

The new agreement with Stalin saw the Soviets grant amnesty to all Polish citizens kept in Soviet prisons, mines and labour camps, with the Polish government-in-exile agreeing to create a Polish Army in the south of the Soviet Union to help fight the German forces.

Tens of thousands of Polish prisoners-of-war were released, with the amnesty also providing the opportunity for the organised flight from exile of deportees in Siberia.

Maria said the 'great news' of the amnesty reached them at the camp in August.

"The men could join the Polish Army to fight the German forces, and we were all free to leave. However every person had to pay 50 rubles to be transported out of the region. Our family didn't have such a sum of money, as both of our parents were too ill to work by then."

Many others in the settlement sold whatever clothing and utensils of value they could muster to raise the money for the journey. However the Węgrzyn family had nothing for sale.

Although Maria had fulfilled her 'norm' of work, she had never been paid. Finally the Russian authorities paid her 400 rubles, which was enough to hire a horse and sleigh to transport the family out of Czary to the nearest railway station, some 35km away.

From there they would journey to Uzbekistan to live in a communist collective.

"By now it was late September, and there was deep snow covering the country, and heavy frosts. It was a long journey and the driver was only able to take Mama and the three youngest, Władzia, Frania and Bronek on the sleigh. The rest of us had to trudge behind, hungry and exhausted. Tata was still quite ill and struggled in the deep snow. I kept an eye on him and the sleigh, which at times got further and further away from us. I feared Tata would fall and die," said Maria.

Other Polish families walked the entire way carrying their possessions on their backs, while some hauled a small sled behind them.

Józefa said with the temperatures continuing to plunge, people were freezing.

"A boy named Tadeusz Olech froze to death on the journey. Mama, holding little Bronek, fell out of the sleigh onto the snow twice. Somehow we all managed to get to the township where the train station was."

The Węgrzyn family lodged with a kind Russian woman in a large room in her home, where they waited a week for the train, which would take them south to what they hoped, was freedom.

Tens of thousands of Polish deportees endured terrible conditions
while being transported in cattle wagons to and from Siberia.

The family's joy at their liberation from Czary was short-lived, when conditions on the train journey south, although bearable at the start, rapidly worsened. They were assigned to cattle wagons with 35 to 40 passengers. But this time, under the care of the Polish authorities, rather than the Soviets, food was supplied frequently to begin with.

"Whenever the train stopped, they handed out bread, soup and sometimes fish. But this did not happen all of the trip," said Józefa.

The journey took them over wide stretches of land with only sparse vegetation. Few towns and villages appeared. Later there were grasslands, with sheep, donkeys and camels grazing. As the train passed through Sverdlovsk, Serov and Chelyabinsk conditions on the train started to worsen. People on board were sick, hungry and filthy, and had to deal with constant lice infestations. Then no supplies of food arrived at all, and many people died in the terrible conditions. One man, Mr Babisz from the family's wagon, fell under the train and lost both his legs. His younger brother died soon after. Several people were left behind at various stations along the route, but most managed to rejoin the group when they reached their final destination.

One day, when the train halted in large rail yards at Tashkent, in Kazakhstan, Maria took a bucket and crawled under the carriages of several lines of trains standing in a maze of railway lines, to search for water.

"No one told us when the train was leaving again. I got back in time, but Tata had gone looking for some bread and other food, and was stranded with the Commandant of Transport when the train departed. Mama and all of us were very worried as to what would befall us without Tata, but thank God, he rejoined our train two days later," said Maria.

During the journey, the family saw many collectives (kolkhoz) where Polish people were already in residence. Some of the new settlers told the deportees on the train that conditions in Uzbekistan were even worse than in Siberia. Some chose not to believe them, while others were comforted by the thought it was at least warmer there than in freezing Siberia. When the train stopped at its final destination in Uzbekistan, and the Polish people saw the wagons ready to transport them, almost all agreed not to leave the train, and to demand to be returned to Tashkent. However the Uzbek communist collective commandant ordered them to get out, otherwise they would not be fed.

"We all cried, 'don't give us any food, just send us back to Tashkent'. Then one Pole got out together with his family and went to the dining hall. He scoffed at us while eating."

When they realised their protests were fruitless, the Poles eventually left the train the following afternoon. They were given some cabbage and seed biscuits to eat and told to load their possessions onto oxcarts. The older Węgrzyn children carried the smaller children on their backs during the 4km journey from the station to Kitab.

It was a small town, close to the Afghanistan border and was surrounded by communist collectives.

The family was given a brief respite at an Uzbek teahouse where they stayed the night, and were given naan bread in the morning. They were taken to a laundry where they steam cleaned their quilts and clothing to get rid of the lice from the train journey.

The Węgrzyns were still with their extended family, but the next day, the rest of the family, apart from Aunty Zosia, Uncle Aleksander and little Maria, were assigned to different collectives. They were separated from their Babcia (grandmother), Aunty Katarzyna Krawiec (née Majda), Uncle Józef Majda, and Aunty Maria, the widow of Uncle Pawel who had perished as they left Siberia.

"The rest of our family was taken in a totally different direction at the crossroads from Kitab. It was a very sad journey and we cried, wondering where they were taking us," said Józefa.

At dusk, they arrived at a kolkhoz named 'Kalinin'. Some Polish people, who had arrived a week earlier, came out to greet them.

"When we inquired about the conditions of life and work, we learned there was much hardship in both."

Kalinin was an eyesore, with huts built from mud and straw, and the lanes between them full of pools of dirty water. A mud wall surrounded each hut. At the entrance to each property was a small toolshed, which was supposed to be used for storing agricultural implements, or keeping a goat. It was in one of these dilapidated huts that the family and the three orphan boys by the name of Żadło, who had been assigned to live with them, were housed. There were no windows, and no stove for cooking or to keep warm.

When the family arrived, it was late evening, and the sun had already set. The cart driver threw their belongings on to the ground and they carried them inside the hut. There were no beds, no table, or anywhere to sit, apart from two shelves on each side of the hut. The family managed to find some boards to sleep on.

In the morning they were given some crude pancakes and told to go to work.

"Maria, our 12-year-old brother Janek, and I were told to uproot cotton bushes and burn them. Each of us was allotted one plot to clear. We all suffered terribly. The cotton bushes were thorny and hard to handle without work gloves. At the end of the day our arms and hands were bleeding. We were hungry when we returned in the evening and given naan bread, baked from dark flour, which looked like clay," said Józefa.

The children had to complete other hard manual tasks, such as carrying earth and manure out on to the fields, pruning, and digging drains.

Józef Węgrzyn was made to work in the forge with two of the children's uncles, making carts, cart wheels, and coke from coal. He even made coffins.

"They received no pay, and were given gritty pancakes mixed with weedy millet to eat, which were distributed each morning and evening, before and after work."

Aniela Węgrzyn had the tedious task of teasing out the cotton buds, which required her to sit in one place all day.

"The work was arduous, yet we received no pay, nor recompense of any sort. Not even rationed bread. We starved," said Maria.

To survive, people who had things to sell would take them to the bazaar in Kitab and buy cabbages, beetroot, carrots, onions, yoghurt, nuts, millet or watermelons. Those who had nothing to sell would try to feed on grass and shrubbery. Many died of starvation.

"We were able to exchange some of our meagre possessions to buy onions and cabbages at the bazaar, and to avoid starvation we started to eat the cotton seeds, which the local Uzbeks would crush for cotton oil, or make into round yellow patties to feed their sheep. When they saw us eating the seeds they warned us not to, as we could die."

Besides the lack of food, there was no clean water at the settlement. The family's only source was from a nearby stream, where the cows trod, and the Uzbek women washed their laundry.

Christmas Day 1941 was sad for the family, as they all had to work, including young Janek. By January, many people at Kalinin had fallen ill with typhoid and died.

"Tata had a very high temperature, and Józefa and Mama were also very ill. I didn't have a fever but was too weak to walk because of the lack of food. I didn't get typhoid because back in Siberia I had been regularly inoculated as one of the workers," said Maria.

Janek reported the family's plight and a local Russian district nurse came and insisted Aniela and Józefa be taken to the hospital at Kitab. She considered Józef Węgrzyn beyond medical help and too ill to go. The next day, Aniela and Józefa were carried out to an oxcart, covered by a quilt, and taken to hospital. Janek made the journey with them.

Maria stayed behind to care for the three younger children and her father. They were all sick and starving.

Józefa said when they arrived at the hospital at Kitab around midday, the rude Uzbek driver drove up to the doors and told them to get off the cart. He turned the oxen straight around and headed for the bazaar, leaving them standing in front of the hospital.

"Janek went into the hospital to enquire if this was the hospital for typhoid patients, and they said, 'No. There is another hospital further on'. We didn't know where to go. Mama was too weak to walk by herself. I began to cry, wondering what to do. Then Janek put the quilt on his back, took Mama with one hand and me with the other, and thus we struggled on. Mama fell into the mud at times and couldn't walk on. I also began to weaken in strength. Janek was at his wits end as to what to do, but somehow we forged on and reached the hospital gates."

A nurse came out, and after reading their medical notes, ushered them into a small room in the hospital. Józefa and her mother were told to undress and put on a short nightdress each. After their hair was cut short they were led to a ward where they were given a rickety bed to share. Then they were given some medicine, covered with a blanket, and left alone.

Janek pulled the quilt back on his back, and after saying goodbye, started the long walk back to Kalinin, without really knowing the way.

"Mama was very worried in case Janek got lost. That night both she and I had a dream that he was drowning while crossing a river, something which very nearly happened. I found out later that an Uzbek man had saved him. On the rest of the way home, Janek stopped to ask for directions and finally returned to our mud hut at Kalinin where everyone lay sick," said Józefa.

Conditions at the hospital were very bad. The food was poor and tasteless, with boiled water and a small piece of dark half-baked bread for breakfast, a small dish of stinking soup for lunch, and more bread for dinner.

"Lots of people died, and the hospital crawled with lice and vermin. The bedding was changed every two months, and the hospital wards were freezing. There was snow outside and regular frosts, yet they never heated the place. Mama and I remained together on one bed, covered with a single blanket. Night times were the worst. We constantly asked for one more blanket, but in vain. Mama's temperature got higher and higher, and she didn't eat all week, surviving on cold water."

Back at Kalinin, Józef Węgrzyn's health was also in decline. He was delirious, with a high temperature and was unable to eat. For four days he still went to work, only to return because he was too weak.

He lay sick for another three days, then on Saturday 7 February 1942, his children woke to find that he had died. His body lay in the hut until the afternoon, as there was no one available to carry it to the local cemetery.

"I was still too weak to walk, enfeebled by starvation. So Janek went to inform the kolkhoz office. It was a depressingly sad time because Mama and Józefa were in hospital and unaware that Tata had died. We also feared Mama may not return to us. We were in deep sorrow," said Maria.

There were few Polish men left to help bury Józef's body, as most had by then enlisted in the Polish Army. Maria said some Uzbek men arrived with sticks and were wailing and yelling at the entrance to the hut, but wouldn't touch the body for fear of getting typhoid.

"Janek had to go out and find a Polish man, and the two of them placed Tata's body on a woven mat given to us by the Uzbeks. Poor Janek, who was only 12 years old, walked behind them and watched the simple burial."

A few days later, the eldest of the three Żadło boys, who was living with the family, also died. He was just 18 years old. Soon after the younger Żadło brothers left the family.

On Tuesday 10 February 1942, Janek bravely walked back to the hospital to inform Józefa and his mother that Józef was dead.

"I got upset and although the nurses tried to calm me down, I didn't stop crying. Mama had such a high temperature that she wasn't even aware of Janek's presence. I didn't tell Mama that Tata had died, because she would not have comprehended it anyway. After a while Janek had to return to Kalinin," said Józefa.

During the following two days, Aniela Węgrzyn lay delirious and moaning. Her body was swollen.

"She constantly begged me to go and buy some red wine. I tried forcefully to go but the nurses wouldn't let me. So I cried all day. I found it intolerable to hear Mama's pleading and I wasn't allowed to do anything. It was an agonising experience. I didn't sleep on the night of Thursday 12 February as I hugged Mama in the hospital bed. All the other patients in the ward were asleep. Mama told me she wouldn't survive the night. It was the worst experience of my life. She died at 10am the next morning, aged just 42."

Until that day, Józefa's health had been improving, but after her mother's death the fever returned. She kept fainting, and in between times, pleaded with the nurses to be allowed to return to her family at Kalinin.

"My clothing was in the hospital storage room, and I cried so much they finally brought it to me. I got dressed and set out, even though my temperature was over 39 degrees. Mama's body still lay on the hospital bed when I left."

It was raining, and Józefa didn't know which direction to go. She fell into the mud and wandered about, crying and soaked through. Finally she met a Polish girl, Bronia Gradzik, who was being driven to join the Polish Army.

"She directed me to the road to Kalinin. When I finally got back there it was dark. I entered the hut crying, and my sisters and Janek surmised that Mama had died. I couldn't speak a word, even though they coaxed me to tell them why I was crying. They tried to console me then everyone started crying, even little Frania and Bronek, although we hadn't told them anything. Aunty Zosia returned from work and no one could speak, but she too concluded that Mama had died. We cried all night until morning. No one went to work, as we were too ill. What great grief was in our hearts. We were orphaned with the deaths of Tata and Mama. If only we had been in Poland. But in Uzbekistan there was no one to work for our family. We were sure death by starvation awaited us all. We had become so weak, we found it difficult to speak. Any day now we might die."

The children's Aunty Zosia, who also lived in Kalinin with her husband and little daughter, Maria, would prove critical to their survival. She was still in reasonable health and had some money from the sale of some clothes at the bazaar in Kitab. Her husband Aleksander Skałka and his brother Jan, had both enlisted in the Polish Army, which was being formed in Uzbekistan. Jan Skałka (whose wife Małgorzata had died of cancer in Siberia) was going to leave his children, Maria and Franek, in Zosia's care

Soon after, a Polish soldier arrived at Kalinin, who told Janek, and Jan Skałka's son, Franek, how to enlist in the Polish Army cadets. Maria was relieved, as she thought Janek would get better care as one of the cadets.

"I was convinced Janek would soon die, as his legs and stomach were swollen from starvation. We were told that such a dire condition meant certain death."

Maria walked with the boys to an army depot around 12km away from Kalinin, to enlist them.

"The boys were exhausted by the long journey, but thank God we got there safely. I was so pleased because I knew Janek would get the medical care he so urgently needed, and the boys would be better fed."

Maria stayed the night at the depot, sleeping on a bare floor mat in a tent in freezing conditions. The next morning a Polish soldier gave her some bread and an empty one litre earthen jar. He told her about a Polish relief centre, in Shaharzab, a town around 12km from Kalinin, where welfare was being given to civilian families. Maria hurried there to get soup for her family. Every day for the next three weeks, she and Józefa would make the long walk to the relief centre together, or would sometimes take turns, to collect the soup. They had to stand in a queue to receive the required coupon, which would entitle them to two cups each. Then they would carefully carry the soup on the long walk back to Kalinin, where their younger siblings were waiting.

There were a few bad mishaps. One day, as Maria and Józefa approached a settlement on the way to Shaharzab, a large dog ran up and bit Maria, causing a deep gash on her leg. She struggled on to the relief centre, but was too injured to return back to Kalinin, so stayed with an aunty overnight. Józefa had to return to Kalinin alone, and on the way back, as she attempted to jump a ditch, slipped and fell into the water, losing all of the soup from the jug.

"I was overwrought with anguish. My siblings were waiting for me and I was returning with an empty jug."

Thanks to the help from the relief centre and Aunty Zosia, the children managed to stay alive, but it was becoming an increasingly impossible burden for Maria and Józefa to look after their younger siblings.

Soon after, while at the relief centre, Maria discovered Polish children could be taken into care at a local orphanage, one of several hastily set up by the Polish authorities after the amnesty, to care for the thousands of Polish children who had lost their families and were trying to head south, either alone or with older siblings. The next day, Maria and Józefa carried Frania and Bronek all the way there.

"When we got to the orphanage, we were all exhausted. Two Polish ladies, dressed in fur coats, answered the door, and told us explicitly they did not accept ill children. I begged them to take Frania and Bronek, pleading they were just exhausted and not ill. In fact they were very ill. Had we not given them into care they would have certainly died of starvation, because no one at the kolkhoz, apart from Aunty Zosia cared for our welfare."

Fortunately Frania and Bronek were taken into care at the orphanage. This meant three of the six Węgrzyn children were now hopefully getting some much needed help.

A couple of days later, Maria and Aunty Zosia went to find the kolkhoz where Zosia's mother, Franciszka Majda (the children's Babcia), and Uncle Jozek Majda, who cared for her, were housed.

"We left early in the morning and that afternoon managed to find Uncle Jozek who told us the sad news that Babcia had died in the Kitab hospital in January, and Maria, Uncle Pawel's widow, had also died in hospital. He said the Polish authorities in Shaharzab were registering family members of Polish soldiers for transport out of Uzbekistan to Persia, so we quickly ran the whole 10km journey there, to ensure we were registered before the office closed at 5pm. Thank God we made it in time. Aunty Zosia registered us all as her own children otherwise we would not have been able to leave the Soviet Union. It was great news but I was worried whether Frania and Bronek would also be transported out of Uzbekistan, now they were in the orphanage. While we were in Shaharzab, for the first time in two years, we attended a celebration of Mass, taken by a Polish Army chaplain."

Józefa remembered coming home from work exhausted after carrying earth all day, and being told by Maria they would be leaving Kalinin the next day.

"I couldn't believe it. We packed our few belongings and in the morning the oxcart came. We arrived at the railway station at midday. The Uzbek driver threw our belongings off the cart onto some large grounds beside the railway. We moved them to the relief centre where we stayed for three days. We received no food until the third day, when we were given bread, sugar, margarine, biscuits and 100 rubles, as there were several of us. Finally we left by train, with Maria, Władzia and I in the same carriage as Aunty Zosia. Uncle Aleksander was in another carriage with the Polish Army volunteers. Our train journey wasn't as sorrowful as our two previous ones to Siberia and Uzbekistan. We were at last leaving a land where we had endured so much suffering, and were heading for Persia."

The family was part of the first stage of evacuations from the Soviet Union, which took place between 24 March and 4 April 1942. Under the orders of General Władysław Anders, 33,069 military personnel and 10,789 civilians including 3100 children were evacuated across the Caspian Sea to Persia (modern day Iran).

A further 69,247 Polish people left the Soviet Union during the second evacuations in August 1942. The 115,742 evacuees who managed to leave the Soviet Union in 1942, were still a small fraction of the approximately 1.2 million Polish citizens who had been deported at the start of the war. Most were forced to stay in the Soviet Union, where the attitude towards Poles continued to worsen as the war went on.

During the three-day trip to Krasnovodsk, on the Caspian Sea, the train stopped at a station where people bought bread, butter, meat and onions. Following their arrival at Krasnovodsk, the family's papers were checked and they were given a meal of fish soup and rice.

On the seashore, they exchanged their Russian currency, and in the evening, Polish soldiers helped them to board a boat for the journey to Persia.

"In the morning we began our journey. It was stormy, with waves tossing the boat. Seawater splashed over us and drenched our clothes, bedding and belongings. Maria, Władzia and I were seasick the whole time," said Józefa.

Early the next day, Holy Saturday 1942, the boat reached the Persian coast. After disembarking, the family was loaded into army vehicles and driven to Pahlavi (now Anzali), which had been set up as a transit camp by the Red Cross and Polish government-in-exile.

"We came to a sandy place, where we unloaded. Army tents were pitched everywhere, with 20 people designated to sleep in each one. We were all so tired, we went straight to rest and sleep," said Józefa.

Persian children moved around the camp wanting to buy clothing from the Polish refugees.

Maria swapped a duvet for four boiled eggs.

Some of the new arrivals had their heads shaved due to lice infestations and disease, however the sisters' hair was just cut short. All of their clothing was processed in a steam disinfecting plant to clean them up and rid them of lice.

The tent city housing Polish evacuees near Tehran

The following morning, the family was delighted to see Polish soldiers had decorated an altar with flowers and greenery, and to discover they would be attending Easter Sunday Mass.

"Each one of us was thanking God for liberating us from slavery. After two years we could once again celebrate the feast of Easter. After Mass the priest blessed the food with the symbolic paschal lamb, Easter eggs, Polish salami and bread. Then, in our traditional Polish custom, we exchanged Easter greetings and shared the Easter eggs. We had a very happy day. That evening we went bathing in a bath house and walked to another tent camp, where we slept under the stars," said Józefa.

The next evening, the family was given a two-day supply of food, consisting of dates, margarine, milk and tinned food, and on the Tuesday morning, boarded a vehicle for the journey from Pahlevi to Tehran.

The roads were rough, narrow and dangerous, winding through the mountains and over treacherous gorges.

Two days later they arrived in Tehran, a city Józefa described as 'large and beautiful'.

"The avenues were lined with trees, and the buildings were made of permanent material with decorative flower bed frontages. There were shops on either side of the streets, which displayed all sorts of merchandise. We quickly passed through the city where Persian people greeted us with flowers, biscuits and cakes."

On their second day in the camp, the family was part of a large group, including Aunty Zosia and several of their old acquaintances from Ostrów and Czary, who were transferred to a building called Block 15. It was a partly completed hangar, hurriedly left by German contractors. Although it lacked windows, the sisters were pleased to have a roof over their heads.

After enduring desperate years of starvation, the sisters were delighted to receive three simple meals a day. For breakfast and dinner they were given bread and tea, and at lunchtime, soup with rice and meat. This was their daily menu for some time.

No one was forced to work, however some of the people in the camp chose to help in the kitchen. Maria worked in the outdoor army kitchen, helping to ladle out servings of thick soup.

"The cooks were young Polish soldiers. They lacked kitchen utensils and large enough knives to carve up the meat, so would throw a whole mutton carcass into a very large cauldron, add a sack full of rice, and boil it up into a thick soup. This was dished out to queues of hungry people, many of whom got sick from eating it. Some even died, as it was too rich and fatty for their starved stomachs to digest."

Healthier children, such as Maria, Józefa and Władzia were sent to schools in the compound, which had been established by the Polish government-in-exile in a bid to help ensure the intellectual, cultural and social development of its vulnerable young citizens.

"It was a very happy time. We attended Polish lessons and took part in staged plays and concerts," said Józefa.

Hospitals had been set up for the weak and sick children who arrived in Tehran, a great many of whom were terribly ill, and lice-infested.

The sisters were eventually moved to Compound 2 with Aunty Zosia, her daughter Maria, and another cousin, Maria Skałka.

At a nearby airbase, the Polish Army cadets had their headquarters, and when the sisters' brother Janek, and cousin Franek Skałka learned of their presence in the refugee camp, they came to visit. They were overjoyed to be reunited.

"We sisters often visited Janek, and he in turn visited us. But in time he and Franek departed for Palestine with the Polish Army cadets," said Józefa.

The sisters were also delighted to learn that the children from the Polish orphanage, which had taken in Frania and Bronek back in Uzbekistan, had been shipped to Persia, and were situated in Compound 1 in their camp, said Maria.

"We were so happy and relieved to know Frania and Bronek were safe. To be reunited with them, the three of us, and our cousin

Janek Węgrzyn in Palestine.
He served with the Polish
Army Cadets from 1942-
1946.

Maria registered to move to Compound 1. Aunty Zosia was most upset, as it meant we would be separated from her. But we so wanted to be with our younger siblings, so had to do this to become part of the orphanage."

On their arrival at the orphanage, the sisters were devastated to be told the children had already moved on.

Frania had been transported with her group of children to the city of Isfahan, more than 400km from Tehran.

Bronek was consigned to a tent hospital beyond the camp confines.

"There were hundreds of sick people and children in the tent hospital, and we were not allowed to go anywhere near it to prevent the spread of serious illnesses," said Maria, who decided to come up with a plan.

Back at the orphanage there were no toilets, with the children having to use toilet buckets instead.

These were regularly emptied into the sand dunes beyond the gates of the camp, which were guarded by Polish soldiers.

"I found another girl who had a sick relative in the tent hospital, and we volunteered to take out the toilet buckets. As soon as we passed the Polish sentry and were out of sight beyond the camp gates, we dumped the buckets. I ran to hospital tent 21 where I knew Bronek was."

When Maria found Bronek, he was in a terrible condition, sitting on a bed, clutching a large toy horse, and begging all who passed to swap the toy for a bucket of soup.

"Bronek didn't recognise me and was thin with hunger. He was being given regular injections and had been put on a strict diet of rusks and tea. He craved some food, and was desperate for some soup."

Józefa also managed to visit Bronek in the tent hospital and was saddened by his condition.

"He was ill in bed, all skinny, and crying bitterly. He complained of the many injection wounds in his legs, and his sore head. I was most upset to see him suffer so. Even though there were toys around he didn't play with them. He kept asking for a drink but the nurse had to keep to the strict diet prescribed by the doctor."

Conditions in the orphanage were comfortable but strict, with the religious brothers and nuns who ran it not allowing the sisters to leave the compound, even if they had a pass.

There was insufficient adult staff to provide adequate care for all of the children, so older girls, such as the Węgrzyn sisters, helped by bringing in the buckets of food, doing the younger children's dishes, and washing their laundry.

Aunty Zosia remained in Compound 2 and continually visited the girls. Some time later, her little girl Maria, aged four years old, died of sunstroke, which was another deeply upsetting loss for the family, said Maria.

"Aunty Zosia was most distressed. She was now alone, having lost her only child. By then Uncle Aleksander was fighting with the Polish Army in Iraq."

After they had been in Tehran for two-and-a-half months, the girls learned they were being transferred to Isfahan, where their little sister Frania was already located.

"On 16 June 1942, a Polish soldier arrived and called out my name. He brought Bronek, who looked a little better, but was still crying. He didn't recognise us as his family. The next day, we all departed to Isfahan, where children who needed the most care were sent."

The heat and lack of water made the two-day journey difficult. As they got closer to Isfahan, they saw undulating hills with fields of wheat and rye, gardens, orchards, and greenery.

Twenty-one compounds had been set up across Isfahan for Polish children, with many affluent families, religious organisations and even royalty, donating their homes, buildings, monasteries and convents to be set up as orphanages, hospitals and schools.

The city took in 2043 children, who were either orphans, or accompanied by one surviving parent. The Węgrzyn sisters were happy to be in such a beautiful city, with its wonderful architecture, wide boulevards, and exotic foods, such as fig, quince and pistachio growing on trees and bushes. Bazaars were formed by long narrow passageways between buildings, with small shops on either side. People would cram into the narrow shopping alleys to buy their goods.

Following their arrival in Isfahan, the sisters' group was met by a Polish professor, named Mr Dymowski, who instructed them all to line up in pairs. The group then met Krystyna Skwarko, a remarkable Polish teacher and humanitarian. She had been director of a Polish children's orphanage in the south of the Soviet Union, and was the founder and director of the Polish homes and schools in Isfahan, which were all funded by the Polish government-in-exile.

Krystyna led the group through the narrow streets of Isfahan until they reached a wide gate, leading to a large building with trees in front of it. This was Compound 6, run by the Armenian religious brothers, which would be the children's short-term home. Once inside the building, the Węgrzyn sisters were shown to a large dormitory, which had beds covered with clean white bedding. It was the first time they had slept on wooden beds since leaving Siberia. The girls were very happy in their new surroundings but missed their Aunty Zosia, said Maria.

"We heard later that Aunty Zosia found her older sister Katarzyna in Tehran, who sadly had lost her son, Wladek, through illness. They remained in Tehran until they were eventually transferred with other Polish refugees to Africa."

After some desperate weeks trying to find out the whereabouts of Frania and Bronek, the sisters finally discovered Frania was in

Compound 10, and Bronek was in a sanitorium in Compound 19 in Isfahan.

"There were no buses available and I had to hire a horse-drawn cab to visit Frania. When we met, she didn't recognise me. She just looked at me, turned around, and walked away," said Maria.

The sisters were saddened to discover Bronek's health had deteriorated in Isfahan, as the nursing staff were unaware of his restricted diet.

"In time a Polish doctor was assigned to the hospital and he succeeded in bringing Bronek back to health."

Bronek (front left standing) with other children in
Persia, after his health improved.

The sisters were happy to be transferred to Compound 9, which was located in the central city area.

"We were excited and eagerly awaited the day of our transfer. After our traditional morning prayers, we had breakfast of two eggs, cheese and a whole pancake, then marched to Compound 9. We were so happy to find a beautiful orchard with a large two-storied building. Lunch was tasty chicken noodle soup with potatoes, meat and sauce for the main course. After the meal we were assigned our dormitories, then had a rest until 4pm, with grapes for our afternoon snack."

Several primary schools and a secondary school were set up in Isfahan, but due to the lack of classrooms, the sisters attended lessons in the orchard to begin with.

"Mrs Figulanska was our teacher. She was very kind to us, like a mother. Our lessons were not like in Poland. We lacked textbooks, exercise books and other school equipment, and learned from the oral accounts of our teachers."

Despite these limitations the children eagerly looked forward to the lessons, said Józefa.

"We thanked God we were no longer in Russia and were free to pray and learn in Polish."

Maria was happy to have the opportunity to be educated, as she had left school back in Poland at just 10 years of age.

Maria and Józefa (back) with Bronek and Frania in
Isfahan, Persia, circa 1942-43.

"I had forgotten by then how to read and write, but we had excellent teachers and I learned a lot. We also had a very good music teacher who taught us singing. We practised in the evenings and our choir sang on solemn occasions, such as the visits of Bishop Gawlina, who was Polish, and Bishop Marina, who was Italian."

The choir also sang for the Masses of Holy First Communion and Confirmation, which Maria enjoyed.

Around this time, Władzia became anaemic, and was taken to the sanitorium in Compound 11, where she stayed for some time.

In addition to her studies, Józefa volunteered to help in the small local hospital.

"Early in the morning I had to sweep two wards and carry three buckets of water in from outdoors to help wash the patients. Then I would serve breakfast and wash their dishes, eat my own quick breakfast, and go off to school. After the lessons and eating my lunch, I would bring in lunch for the patients, then wash the dishes and sweep the floor. We had a siesta rest until 4pm, when it was time to do school homework. There were always other distracting duties, like cleaning, or knitting to do. Time passed quickly during the day so I would usually study in the evenings, until dark."

Later, when Józefa attended Polish high school classes in another compound, Maria took over her nursing chores.

Scouts and Girl Guides were popular activities at Isfahan, which Józefa, in particular took to with relish.

"Mr Dymowski organised the Girl Guides movement. He bought four Girl Guide banners, with Father Tomasik, our chaplain funding the rest. The girls took turns embroidering the banners, sewing day and night, in preparation for them to be blessed, along with our beautiful flag, made by Mrs Zajdlowa and Mrs Solowiej."

On the day of the blessing the girls marched to a decorated altar in a large park in Compound 1.

A guard of honour stood to attention on either side of the altar with the flag, alongside the Girl Guide leaders holding their banners.

"We turned to look at the Blessed Virgin on the flag, as she sorrowfully gazed upon this Polish nation, dispersed throughout the world. Our hearts filled with ardent prayers to God for our speedy return to our free Fatherland."

A technical school, which trained women in tailoring, was also set up in Isfahan to assist the refugees. Maria applied for a tailoring course, but the quota was full. Instead, the director of the Polish orphanages, Krystyna Skwarko, selected Maria to be one of 16 older Polish girls to learn Persian carpet making with an expert Persian weaver. These methods were normally kept secret, however the rules had been relaxed due to the war and the girls were taught the traditional process.

Maria (top row left) with a group of Polish girls who were taught traditional Persian weaving in Isfahan, 1944.

Maria said the Iranian weaver was a demanding but excellent teacher and a good man.

"Seven out of the 16 girls who made the carpets had lost parents in Russia. We were split into four groups, with each group given a carpet to create. It was tedious work. Mrs Skwarko wanted us to gift the carpets to the Polish President in Exile, Mr Mikolajczyk, who was visiting us. We had to work in two shifts to get them finished, including by lamplight well into the night. Our teacher would become displeased if we made any mistakes, as he was the only one who could correct them."

Some of the rugs were later displayed at the Sikorski Institute in London.

In August 1944, Maria was assigned to work as a caregiver in Compound 10 looking after a group of young boys, among them, her brother Bronek.

"Amongst the orphans was a group of spoiled boys I called 'mummy's darlings', as their mothers worked elsewhere. I had difficulty controlling them. They slept in rows beside each other and were difficult to settle down to sleep."

People staying in Compound 10 were housed in beautiful buildings with large rooms and decorated ceilings with painted birds. However there was no furniture.

"The floors were covered with beautiful Persian carpets, on which local people would sit, eat and sleep. The climate was warm, hence Persian people had no need of bedding. Their gardens and orchards were a delight. They had irrigation channels, which were filled with water each evening, helping them to produce plentiful crops."

By this time, the Węgrzyn family had been in Persia for more than two years and were grateful for the friendliness, kindness and generosity of their caregivers and the local people. People were constantly moving between the compounds in Isfahan, with some refugees departing for overseas as their health recovered.

The intention was never for the Polish people to stay in Soviet-controlled Persia for too long, given the hostility of the Soviet authorities towards the Poles, and the increasing threat from the German armies.

Persia was to prove their gateway to other parts of the world. The Polish deportees were transported to various countries in the

British Commonwealth, including South Africa, Kenya, India, Canada, and New Zealand. This initiative was on the understanding the Poles would be guests of these countries, and would return home to a free Poland, and their surviving family members, at the end of the war.

Late in 1944, plans were underway for the Węgrzyn children to be part of a group of 733 children and 105 caregivers to travel to New Zealand, at the invitation of its Prime Minister, the Rt Hon. Peter Fraser.

The idea had come from Countess Maria Wodzicka, wife of the Polish Consul in New Zealand, who was said to have first shared it with Peter Fraser's wife.

The Węgrzyn children in Persia in 1944, not long
before they left for New Zealand. Józefa and Maria
(back), Frania, Bronek and Władzia.

Krystyna Skwarko, director of the Polish orphanages in Isfahan was to travel to New Zealand to become head of the boys' primary school at the new camp for the Polish children, which was being set up at Pahiatua, around two hours north of Wellington, in the North Island.

Maria was included in the group of 105 caregivers, and assigned to assist Mrs Stanislawa Lewandowska to look after the youngest group of children, aged four to six years old, which included little Bronek. Józefa, Władzia and Frania were also chosen as some of the 733 children to make the journey.

The large group bound for New Zealand was taken to Tehran, then by bus to Basra where they were housed in tents for several days. After being taken by train to Ahwaz, in the Persian Gulf, they boarded a British merchant ship named *Sontay*.

"We were accommodated in a huge cargo hold, empty except for a large pile of dirty mattresses. These infested mattresses caused eye infections in some of the children, including Bronek," said Maria.

Maria and Mrs Lewandowska had 28 children under their care. They had to haul all their food and water into the cargo hold in buckets.

"We used the water to wash the dishes and do the laundry. Since it was so hot the boys ran around in just their shorts. Poor Mrs Lewandowska had to search the decks looking for the ever elusive boys."

Maria kept good health on the voyage and was never seasick. She was so busy she didn't see Józefa, Władzia or Frania on board at all.

After a week they reached India, where it was extremely hot. At Bombay (now Mumbai) they boarded the USS *General Randall*, for the voyage to New Zealand. It was a high-risk journey, which had to be carefully navigated, given the number of Japanese submarines in the Pacific region.

"We had much better conditions on this ship, with large clean cabins, hammocks, and generous navy rations for food. Unfortunately I was seasick, and so ill at times I had to crawl around to do my chores, and wash the boys' clothing. The soldiers on board the ship were very kind, playing with the children and sharing their rations with them."

Maria slept in a hammock next to a girl named Zosia Matula who had tuberculosis in her lungs and cried constantly from the pain.

"There didn't seem to be medical staff on board capable of helping her, so I had to care for her, even though she wasn't in our group."

The ship was led in a naval convoy of four ships, which sailed around Australia, southwards on the western coast and eastwards along the southern coast to avoid Japanese warships in the Pacific war zone. During the evening of 31 October 1944, after six long weeks at sea, the *General Randall* arrived safely in the Port of Wellington, New Zealand.

"It was evening, and there were only a few lights shining because of the wartime blackout restrictions. The next morning, the New Zealand Prime Minister, Peter Fraser and Countess Maria Wodzicka came on board to officially greet us. We were delighted to disembark and stand on firm ground again in such a beautiful country with friendly people."

Polish refugee children arriving at Pahiatua Railway Station. *Photographer: Pascoe, John Dobree, Ref:1/2-003646-F. Courtesy of Alexander Turnbull Library, Wellington, New Zealand*

The large group was transferred to a passenger train, which was stationed next to the ship, and taken to the town of Pahiatua.

The Polish Children's Camp in Pahiatua had been established around 3km south of the Pahiatua township, on land which had originally been a racetrack, formed in 1901.

During World War II, an internment camp had been built on the site with barracks and buildings to accommodate enemy nationals.

When it was converted for the purpose of housing the Polish children, street names were added bearing Polish names, with Polish primary and secondary schools established.

The Polish government-in-exile initially contributed funds to help pay for the children's care at Pahiatua, but eventually full responsibility was taken over by the New Zealand Government, with the camp administered by the New Zealand Army. A hospitality committee had been set up in New Zealand, which ensured the camp was tidied, beds made, and flowers were put on the tables ready for the children's arrival. Maria said the group received a wonderful welcome in New Zealand.

"It was a beautifully fine day. At all the stations we passed, children, who had been given time off school to greet us, were waving, with flags flying in both New Zealand and Polish colours. Some of the Polish children screamed when we travelled through the Manawatu Gorge, as they were frightened to see the steep high riverbanks."

During one stop, at Palmerston North, the mayor and some local citizens handed the children ice creams.

"As a caregiver of the youngest children I was given a big box of ice creams, and when we arrived at the Pahiatua camp, I had no opportunity to find a proper refrigeration place to store them. I placed the box under my bed in the boys' dormitory. In the morning there was a river of melted ice cream flowing under the beds. I had yet another cleaning chore that day."

With so many young charges to care for, Maria said there was no let up of work for her once they reached the camp.

"I arrived with five huge bundles of dirty washing, wrapped in sheets, which took me two days to wash. There were no organised staff for the laundry, so we caregivers washed all the clothes, and the bedding of the children who regularly wet their beds."

At the camp, Maria was reappointed to her job as caregiver of the preschoolers, along with house mother, Mrs Lewandowska, kindergarten teacher, Mrs Rubisz, and administrator, Mrs Tietze. Preschoolers were assigned to a large block, which had around 56 beds.

The building was divided down the middle by the caregivers' rooms, with boys sleeping on one side and girls on the other.

Although Maria had her own room, she chose to sleep in the dormitory with the 20 boys she was tasked with looking after, as many of them had chilled bladders and needed her help to go to the toilet when they woke during the night.

Maria, with Major Foxley, Mrs Lewandowska and young Polish boys at Pahiatua, 1945.

Given what they had been through in Poland and Russia, many of the boys had severe problems. Maria said she was always haunted by the memory of the small children in her care crying in their sleep, possibly dreaming of their lost mothers.

The camp was run military style under the administration of the New Zealand Army, with a hooter signalling the children's daily programme. Although it was helpful to have a strict routine, it also created stress for the caregivers, said Maria.

"The children had to wake on the first hooter, and by the second hooter we had to have them up, washed and dressed, with their boots laced and morning prayers said, ready to be marched to the dining hall. Only half an hour was allowed for the meal. I had to take all the children's plates to the table, and some of them would just sit and stare at the plate. I didn't always get them all fed."

Maria's duties also included washing the young boys' dishes and supervising the older boys who were rostered to wash the dishes of around 180 older children assigned to the dining hall, once they had finished eating. Sometimes they gave Maria the slip and she had to wash all the dishes herself.

"The army boss would come and run his fingers across the plates. If he found any grease the dishes would all have to be washed again."

Caregivers also had to make the beds, clean the shower and toilet block, and sweep the floors. Then there was lunch and dinner to feed the boys, baths, helping them into their pyjamas and trying to settle them into bed.

Maria worked seven days a week, with no days off. Her only break was when the children were taken to the hall to watch a film and she would enjoy some peace and quiet and do some embroidery. She needed permission to go shopping in Pahiatua and didn't venture there often.

"I didn't have time to make friends as all my time went into caring for the children. In some ways I was like a mother to all those little boys."

With life so all-consuming in the camp, it took time for Maria to adjust to life in New Zealand. Most of the lessons in the camp were in Polish, with only a handful of English lessons each week. There were few opportunities to mix with the local people, as it was still expected the Poles would return home at the end of the war.

"It was hard for quite a while to find out what you are supposed to do and who you belonged to. I was lucky that a New Zealand girl who used to visit me at the camp asked me to spend Christmas with her family. There were about 12 children and they had an American mother. It was wonderful."

While life was hard for Maria as a caregiver at the Polish Children's Camp, her younger sisters Józefa and Frania fared better as part of the group of children in the camp's care.

Józefa spent a year in a senior class at the camp and enjoyed being part of a lively, close-knit group. Some of her favourite memories of camp life included performing in plays and nativity scenes, and leading a Girl Guides group.

Youngest sister Frania had happy memories of arriving at Pahiatua camp as an eight year old. She and Bronek stayed at the camp until it closed in 1949.

"Life was good because we never had to worry about food, we had our own beds, and everything was clean. There were also lots of other children to play with. I remember playing American baseball, horse riding for the first time, and climbing and sliding down pine trees. We did marching, and slept in big dormitories. I remember going into the library at the camp and talking to a chap who said how wonderful it was to read and how it opened up your mind. That really touched me and I was a bookworm for years. We used to have lights on in the dormitory at night, and I would spend most of the night reading. I loved it so much. Pahiatua was so good to us. We had some wonderful, dedicated teachers. One of them even took me away on a holiday."

Frania said she and Bronek were lucky to have their older sisters with them in New Zealand, as some of the children were completely on their own.

"One of my good friends at Pahiatua, who later became a school-teacher, had nobody. We were a very lucky family."

Frania (second row, third from right) in her English class at
Pahiatua, with teacher Mr McKinnon.

Frania had only vague memories of her early life in Russia and
Persia.

"I think I put it all out of my mind. I do have a vague recollection
of being in a train and putting my hand on a formation of ice, which
looked like little trees, but that is about all. In Persia I remember the
lovely houses the Persians let us live in, and eating beautiful food like
pomegranates and oranges."

L ife for the Polish people left behind in the Soviet Union
didn't improve throughout the war. In March 1940, Stalin
had ordered the 'liquidation' of over 15,000 Polish officers being
held in Russian prisoner-of-war camps. The bodies of over 4000 of
these unfortunate men, bound and shot in the back of the head,
were uncovered by the invading Germans in a mass grave in the
Katyn Forest near Smolensk in 1943. The fate of thousands of
other Polish prisoners-of-war and political prisoners who disappeared is not known. Many of the vanished Poles included top

Polish Army officers, political leaders, government officials and intellectuals.

The Kaytn revelations would prove the breaking point for Soviet and Polish wartime diplomacy.

The Polish Prime Minister in exile, General Sikorski, refused to accept Stalin's claim the atrocity had been carried out by the Germans. The Soviets accused the government-in-exile of cooperating with Nazi Germany and broke off diplomatic relations. General Sikorski was killed in a plane crash, possibly in suspicious circumstances, in July 1943 as he was returning from the Middle East. No subsequent Polish leader would have similar sway with the western Allied politicians, who were not prepared to let the growing Polish-Soviet crisis threaten their cooperation with the Soviet Union.

Meanwhile the barbaric treatment by the Germans in Poland continued unabated.

In addition to their ethnic cleansing regime, which resulted in the deaths of millions of Polish Jews and citizens, the German occupiers set out to abolish culture and religion in Poland, destroying many cultural and educational institutions, museums and churches. Among their targets were the Polish intellectual and political elite, intelligentsia, clergymen, and nuns, who were murdered, sent to concentration camps, or forced into labour.

By the end of World War II, around six million Polish citizens had perished during the occupation by the Soviet Union and Nazi Germany, which equated to around one-fifth of the country's pre-war population.

Poland's formal sovereignty was re-established by a Soviet-formed provisional government at the end of the war, but it remained under military occupation for many years. With Eastern Poland incorporated into the USSR following the Yalta Agreement in 1945, it became apparent the Pahiatua children had no home to go back to in Poland. The New Zealand Government began putting plans in place to give the children permanent residency.

In May 1945, the new Guardianship Council for the Polish children in New Zealand was established and the children were prepared for their new lives. English lessons were intensified.

In early 1945, one of the first groups of Polish girls left the Pahiatua camp to attend New Zealand secondary schools, with a second group of boys and girls leaving in 1946 to join Catholic boarding schools or to go to towns to learn various trades. Boarding hostels in Wellington and Hawera provided accommodation.

In both 1947 and 1948, the communist Warsaw regime, which was dominated by the Soviet Union, demanded the children should be returned to Poland, but the New Zealand Government refused. The children's future in their new country was secured.

Maria worked at the Pahiatua camp until 6 February 1946. By then all of the young preschool boys in her care were at primary school.

"I had to leave the camp and seek work and lodgings in Wellington. I was with four other young Polish ladies who lodged at the Oriental Bay Hostel for Girls, which was state owned. It was very lonely to leave the completely Polish-speaking environment at the camp and move into a totally English-speaking world. We missed our families and the customary lifestyle in the camp. A French lady named Madame Malampre helped us to learn English and sort out some of our problems, but she didn't fully understand our situation and longing for our family and friends back at Pahiatua."

Times were difficult in post-war New Zealand, however work was found for the young women in clothing factories.

They were paid a relatively low wage, and there wasn't a lot left over for personal expenses and clothing, once they had paid their board and transport on the tram.

Maria and the other young women could only stay at the hostel for six months, to allow other young people coming to Wellington to work.

Maria found private board with a 'kind couple' named Mr and Mrs Escott in Kilbirnie, whose adult children had by then, left home.

The Węgrzyn sisters in 1948, from left, Maria, Frania,
Władzia and Józefa.

She was sad to leave behind her two close friends, Rozalia
Manterys and Wiktoria Wypych, who she had lived with at both the
Pahiatua camp and the Oriental Bay Hostel for Girls.

"When we were at the hostel, Wiktoria had given me the address
of her eldest brother Janek Wypych who had served overseas with the
Polish Army, and asked if I would correspond with him. We wrote for
two years before he came out to New Zealand in 1948."

The survival story of Janek Wypych and his family, and their
eventual settlement in New Zealand was incredibly similar to that of
the Węgrzyn family.

In February 1940, together with their parents, Antoni and
Wiktoria Wypych and 11 brothers and sisters, young Janek and
Wiktoria had been wrenched from their home by gun-wielding
Russian soldiers and forced to make the treacherous journey to a
small settlement called Yurochta, in the north of Russia, close to the
Arctic Circle.

The family was at Yurochta for a year, during which time two of the young children died in the terrible conditions. After the Russian amnesty the family joined other Poles in the journey south, stopping at various camps before reaching Kitab, where Antoni and Wiktoria were struck down with typhoid and hospitalised. Around this time, Janek and two of his brothers joined the Polish Army, with two younger brothers joining the cadets. Then Janek became sick with typhoid and was close to death for several weeks. After his recovery he discovered his father Antoni had also recovered from typhoid, and had joined the Polish Army, along with another of Janek's brothers, and a sister Hania.

The enlisted members of the Wypych family joined the new Polish Army in Kazakhstan-Guzari, while the remaining children were sent to Persia. They were overjoyed to hear that their mother, Wiktoria Wypych, would be able to leave Russia and reunite with them in Tehran, where she would recuperate in hospital. However their happiness on their mother's arrival in Tehran was short-lived, as typhoid and severe malnutrition had taken too much of a toll, and she died in hospital.

After joining the Polish Army, Janek was separated from his father, brothers and sister, and was sent to Kanakin in Iraq to learn to drive trucks and armed vehicles, and train in the use of guns and other arms. Two months later, he was sent to Palestine, and was later posted to Egypt, then Italy. His main role in the army was vehicle maintenance, which suited his character, as he didn't like being a soldier.

Meanwhile, six of his younger siblings were sent to New Zealand at the same time as the Węgrzyn children, settling at the Pahiatua camp. At the end of the war, Janek was sent to England with his regiment rather than going back to Poland. He was homesick and missed his family, but enjoyed his correspondence with Maria Węgrzyn, his Polish penfriend in New Zealand. He was also eager to be reunited with his brothers and sisters and arrived in New Zealand in 1948. His father Antoni, and all of his surviving brothers and sisters also settled in New Zealand after the war.

Love quickly blossomed between Janek Wypych and Maria Węgrzyn, and they were married on 2 February 1950, in Wellington. They had five children. Janek worked for years doing tram and bus maintenance. He also owned a fish and chip shop with one of his brothers, and he and Maria ran a sandwich shop in Vivian Street. Maria was well known for her seamstress skills, and made all of her own clothes and the children's school uniforms.

Their home was full of love and laughter and was a hub for their rapidly growing extended families on both sides. There were many dinners, celebrations, and card games, which went late into the night. Maria was happy to spend a lot of time in the kitchen, feeding and caring for her guests.

Another to arrive in New Zealand in 1948 was brother, Janek Węgrzyn, which was an exciting occasion for the family. Once his service ended with the Polish Army, he had been sent back to England, and started corresponding with his brothers and sisters in New Zealand, before making the long journey to be reunited with them.

He was one of many Polish ex-servicemen and relatives of the Pahiatua children to arrive in New Zealand in the late 1940s on the invitation of the New Zealand Government.

In 1948, many of the new arrivals formed the Polish Association, based in Wellington, to help the Polish migrants transition to life in New Zealand. Many were in a vulnerable state, having lost their families, their country, and in many cases, their confidence.

The Polish Association provided a much-needed sense of togetherness, as well as leadership, assistance, and a place where members could meet and continue to foster their Polish culture.

Janek's arrival cleared up a mystery for Frania and Bronek, who had arrived in New Zealand without birth certificates.

"I had always thought I was born on 12 August, and Bronek on 16 July, but when Janek arrived he told us it was the other way around, so we swapped birthdays," said Frania.

Romance was soon in the air for Janek, when he met his sister

Władzia's best friend, Maria Najbert, a beautiful blue-eyed, Polish girl, who had also been at the Pahiatua camp.

The couple married, settled in Wellington and had three children. Janek was an excellent engineer and technician who was known for his attention to detail. He had a great career in civil aviation, working in aircraft maintenance, and was a technician for Kodak, repairing and maintaining cameras used in professional filming.

Throughout his life, Janek was very involved with the Polish Association in Wellington. He passed away in November 2013.

After her year at the Pahiatua camp, Józefa was sent to Sacred Heart College in Christchurch, where she spent a year before starting her nursing training. She did her general training at Masterton Public Hospital so she could be close to Frania and Bronek, who were still being cared for at Pahiatua.

Although Józefa found learning English time consuming and difficult, she did well in her studies and later graduated from her maternity studies at Hastings Public Hospital with an award. Living in the Nurses' Home and attending social dances and Nurses' Balls brought some lighthearted fun into her life.

It was at a Nurses' Ball that Józefa met her future husband, Peter Berry, a patent lawyer. They were married in 1952 and had five children.

During her nursing career, Józefa worked in several hospitals, mainly in Christchurch and Wellington. She particularly enjoyed the 12 years she spent as a staff nurse in the fracture clinic at Lower Hutt Hospital, where she could be closer to her family and the Polish community.

Józefa reluctantly retired when she reached the compulsory retirement age of 60, and focused on her family and gardening.

Although he was not Polish, Józefa's husband Peter had a long-standing interest in Polish history and culture, and learned to speak the language fluently after meeting Józefa. He was very active amongst the Polish community in Wellington.

In 1997, Peter was awarded the Polish Medal of Honour by the post-communist Polish Government for his services to Poland in support of the Polish workers' Solidarity Movement against communist domination, especially in helping to organise the Food for Poland Appeal in the early 1980s.

When Frania left the Pahiatua camp, she attended St Mary's College in Wellington, where she passed School Certificate and University Entrance.

"My English wasn't very good after just one lesson a day at Pahiatua. I will always remember arriving at my new boarding school, with my luggage in hand. The girls, for some reason, kept coming up and asking why I didn't have a nightgown or dressing gown. They were fascinated by my accent and just wanted to hear me speak in English."

Frania did very well at the College, but didn't enjoy it quite as much as life at Pahiatua.

"I would have preferred to have been a day girl at St Mary's and stayed at a Polish hostel with some of the other students, but it didn't happen. However, the nuns were good, life was good, and we got lots of bread and butter."

At Christmastime 1953, a couple of months before Frania was due to begin her studies at Victoria University, she had planned to travel to Auckland with her older sister Władzia, who after leaving Pahiatua, had attended St Mary's College in Mt Albert and was by this time working and boarding privately in the city.

"We tried to book the train on Christmas Eve, but it was full so we had to go after Christmas instead. The train on Christmas Eve ended up crashing at Tangiwai, and 151 people died. We often talked about it afterwards. Obviously we weren't meant to go."

Two handsome young Dutch men boarded at the same place as Władzia, and she eventually married one of them, a man named Hubert Strack. Władzia and Hubert settled in South Auckland, where they raised a large family of seven children. They were very active amongst the Pacific Island community in South Auckland, carrying out a considerable amount of charitable and social work.

In 1954, Frania commenced a Bachelor of Arts degree at Victoria University and although she passed her other subjects, failed the compulsory fifty per cent pass rate in English.

Discouraged, and not realising there might be help available to her, Frania decided to give up university and applied to work in an office instead.

Through one of her workmates, she met a young man named Michael Quirk, who she later married. The couple saved hard and took on additional part-time jobs before buying a dairy at Khandallah, which set them up financially. They had three children.

During a trip to England in 1978, Maria, Frania and Józefa visited their Aunty Zosia and Uncle Aleksander who had both survived the war. Like so many other Poles, they made their home in England. Frania said they lived a good life and had a lovely home.

"We had so much to thank Aunty Zosia for. She was so important in our lives, as we would never have all ended up together in Persia if she hadn't said we were her children."

The sisters also met up with their cousin Franek, who had fought with their brother Janek in the Polish Army. He too, had survived the war and settled in England.

In the 1980s, Frania decided to go back to university and complete her degree. She graduated with a Bachelor of Arts in 1985.

"We were already successful, but for me it seemed like unfinished business. The process of achieving my degree gave me even more satisfaction than the result. We encouraged our three children to study and they all gained university degrees."

After leaving Pahiatua when the camp closed in April 1949, Bronek went with a group of the remaining youngest boys to be cared for at the Polish Boys' Hostel in Hawera. In the 1950s he boarded at St Patrick's College in Silverstream.

Bronek later studied to be a priest in Rome, and served 25 years as a priest in Australia and New Zealand in various capacities including Hospital Chaplain, Polish Chaplain (New Zealand), Chaplain for the Deaf, and Parish Priest.

Between 2007 and 2011, Bronek undertook the significant task of translating Józefa's wartime diary, which she wrote in 1942 in an old Persian exercise book, while in Isfahan, Persia. He also transcribed and translated audio recordings made by Maria in Polish during the 1990s. Both these documents were a valuable resource, which preserved the family's incredible history.

Bronek (left) visiting Aunty Zosia, Uncle Aleksander, and their daughter Krystyna, in London in the 1960s.

Although a small community in New Zealand, the Polish people made their mark on their new homeland becoming good citizens who contributed in many aspects of life. There were significant challenges and it wasn't an easy transition from Poland to life in New Zealand, which had a different language and culture that was difficult to understand. However a great many of the Polish migrants made a real success of their lives in New Zealand. They supported each other and maintained their own culture and special traditions, an important part of their identity. Most of all, they retained their 'Polishness'.

Gerald O'Brien, who was Prime Minister Fraser's electorate secretary and chairperson, and later treasurer of the Polish Hostel Board, said in a commentary that the Polish character melded well with that of New Zealanders.

"They humbly and freely offered to New Zealand their rugged Polish character, that 'vital spark of heavenly flame', adapted to New Zealand's way of life and contributed to it grandly in all walks."

For all six of the Węgrzyn children to survive after losing their parents and enduring such extreme hardship, persecution, sickness, and near starvation during World War II, was an extraordinary feat in itself. Let alone them all finding their way to New Zealand, a tiny island nation at the bottom of the world, whose humanitarian efforts provided them, and many other Polish people, with a safe haven and a new life away from the horrors of war.

The family's story is testament to their incredible will to survive and a determination to stay together at all costs.

The Węgrzyn siblings in 1993, from left, Janek, Józefa, Frania, Władzia, Maria and Bronek.

At just 15 years old, eldest sister Maria Węgrzyn was forced to do the arduous work of an adult in the forests of Siberia, then take on the responsibility as head of the family after her parents' deaths in Uzbekistan.

Her inner strength, courage, and unwavering faith in the face of incredible odds was truly admirable.

As a caregiver in the Pahiatua camp, life was much different for Maria than it was for her sisters and brother.

While she didn't have to worry about life's basic necessities such as food and a roof over her head, and there were no longer threats to her safety, Maria worked day and night, seven days a week, while looking after the little Polish boys at the camp, all of whom had arrived in New Zealand without their parents.

Maria was like a surrogate mother to many of those young boys, with some keeping in touch with her throughout their lives.

In 2017, the Polish RSA awarded Maria the Cross of Merit for her dedication and hard work looking after the Polish orphans.

It was a fitting honour, for a woman, an orphan herself, who had endured so much, yet constantly put her own suffering aside to provide comfort and service to so many others in their time of need.

5

HARRY

WHEN WAR WAS DECLARED on 1st September 1939, Harry Spencer was among 16 young men from Blenheim, a small town at top of the South Island, in New Zealand, who rushed straight away to enlist.

But his enthusiasm was dashed, when unlike the rest of his mates, Harry failed the medical test due to having high blood pressure.

"I was given a V badge to say I had volunteered but that was not good enough for me. My friends had all gone to war and I wanted to catch up with them," said Harry.

This determination finally saw Harry accepted into the army, but not without a little fudging of the rules. When the 2nd New Zealand Division was being formed, a doctor Harry knew managed to convince the recruiters he was fit to fight, without having to undergo a medical.

This was the beginning of Harry's extraordinary service as soldier

No. 21981 in the 2nd New Zealand Divisional Cavalry, or Div Cav as it was known, which was at the sharp end of some of the war's fiercest fighting.

The brave men in this light armoured, forward reconnaissance regiment were sent ahead to explore new territory, and at the end of each battle, were often the last to leave. They carried out some incredibly dangerous work, such as gathering intelligence, and relaying orders and communications in the heat of the battle.

Harry's four years as a soldier would become woven into New Zealand's military history. He was in the first unit of the 2nd Division to engage the enemy in Northern Greece in 1941.

From then on, he took part in almost relentless action, fighting on the battlefields of Greece, Crete, North Africa and the Middle East, and enduring a harsh winter campaign in Italy before being reluctantly sent home at the start of 1944.

The highlight of Harry's service was being part of General Freyberg's Protective Troop, a small group of loyal men with three Stuart tanks and a petrol and ammunition truck, who accompanied Freyberg during the pursuit of German Field Marshal Erwin Rommel's forces from El Alamein to Tripoli during the Desert War.

When aged in his nineties, Harry was honoured to discover he was likely to be the only New Zealand serviceman still living who had fought in every major battle the New Zealanders had engaged in while in Europe, North Africa and the Middle East.

Despite being in the thick of all this action, Harry managed to get through the war almost completely unscathed, with just one small nick to his ear.

However the emotional toll of living through the horrors of battle and losing so many valued friends was a different proposition.

"War was a hell of a thing," he said.

Harry said his Kiwi 'number eight wire' mentality and practicality were two things that got him through many hair-raising and challenging times during the war, skills he had developed while growing up on the family farm at Blenheim.

He made his entrance into the world in July 1916, the third child in his family, following two older sisters, Constance (Connie) and Vera. Harry's English father had arrived in New Zealand in the early 1890s with his two brothers, sharing just three halfpennies between them.

When Harry was young, his father had drawn a ballot for a farm at Ward, in Marlborough, but decided the property wasn't big enough, so drew again and ended up with a 100-acre dairy farm in the same region. Harry's father was a creative man who played many musical instruments and was 'mixed up' with both a circus and an orchestra. His passion for music was always far greater than his love for his cows, which meant young Harry had to help his hardworking mother and sisters do most of the farm work.

Harry (front middle) with his parents, and sisters Connie (left) and Vera.

"By the time I was 17, I was doing all the ploughing and made all the hay. I'm not sure Dad even knew how to hitch up the horse team."

Harry and his two sisters were also musical, although none of them learned to read music.

"I started on the baritone then played third cornet for a while until I had all my teeth out. Then I went to the E flat bass. I played in a brass brand and the conductor never picked up that I couldn't read music."

From a young age, Harry had a quick wit and confident personality, and was adored by his parents (known to all as 'Ma' and 'Pa') and his sisters. When they were teenagers, Connie and Vera played a prank on Harry, which had some unfortunate consequences. After finding some of Harry's home brew hidden in a garden hedge, and knowing he would be unlikely to share it with them, the girls thought it would be funny to taint the beer with Epsom salts. What they didn't realise, was just how ill with diarrhoea Harry and his friends would be for days after drinking it.

Growing up on the farm provided Harry with some handy practical skills like shooting, driving, and fixing vehicles and machinery, which would hold him in good stead during the war.

At the age of 18, he joined the Mounted Rifles with some of his friends, not to be a 'brave soldier' but to be presented with a rifle, so he could go deer stalking and pig hunting.

"We were volunteers and had to go into camp once a year. To us it was a paid holiday even if some of the officers took it seriously."

Harry worked on the construction of the South Island main trunk railway line until he enlisted and was finally accepted into the New Zealand Army. At Christmas time 1939, when he was aged 23, Harry was sent to Papakura Military Camp. His practical and mechanical skills were soon recognised and honed by his regiment, the 2nd New Zealand Divisional Cavalry, and he was schooled up on radio and transport operations.

"Our unit was C Squadron and I was posted to Number One Troop, where I was fortunate to be with one of the best officers in the army, Lieutenant Ian Bonifant. When the Bren gun carriers arrived, I was given a job driving one. It suited me fine. I was Bonny's driver and it started a great friendship."

On his final leave before departing for war, Harry went home to Marlborough and helped to arrange the sale of his father's farm.

"Dad's health was not the best so I helped him sell the farm. Unfortunately that was the last time I saw him. My parents shifted to Blenheim after I sailed and he died while I was in the desert."

Harry and the rest of the Second Echelon of New Zealand troops departed on 1 May 1940 on the 'good ship *Aquitania*', a 45,000 ton liner, the biggest most of them had ever seen. The ship was originally destined for Egypt but was diverted at South Africa for Scotland. As the ship left Freetown, in South Africa, it was joined by the aircraft carrier *Hermes*, and later by HMS *Hood*, and other cruisers. This made war seem closer to the young New Zealanders.

"We sailed through flotsam which had been caused by submarine activity. Anyone who said he didn't have a touch of fear was a liar. But we had faith in our escorts."

The *Aquitania* arrived at Greenock, Scotland the day France capitulated to the Germans. The New Zealanders were deployed to defend the south-eastern coast of England, arriving at Ash Vale Station in Surrey in the early hours of the morning, then marching to Mytchett Woods where they camped in bell tents among pine trees housing squirrels and wood pigeons.

"The next night a stick of bombs was dropped through the camp but the only damage was a hole in the top of the cook's tent," said Harry.

A few days later some worn out tanks and Bren gun carriers arrived, and the regiment was visited by King George VI, British Prime Minister Winston Churchill, and Foreign Secretary Anthony Eden. The soldiers were lined up in a paddock with the tanks when the VIPs arrived. The King stepped out of his car and Kiwi soldier Tommy Bradford, who had been determined to speak with him, was first in line.

"His Majesty went over and shook hands with Tom and the conversation turned to horses. They were both knowledgeable on the subject and had a good talk, which took up most of the King's time. He quickly walked around the rest of us and didn't shake hands with anyone else. After the war Tom would visit me about once a year and always dined out on that story."

With a German invasion of Britain becoming increasingly likely, the New Zealand troops were shifted to the Maidstone area in Kent, where they camped in a pine forest with their vehicles. The weather was bad and many of them ended up with influenza. Harry and one of his best army mates, Allan Risk, ran a temporary hospital for the minor cases but were soon struck down too. They spent a week in an army hospital set up in Viscount Rothermere's nearby manor house, and when they recovered, managed to convince their Major to let them take the leave that was owing to them for a quick trip to Durham to see some people Harry knew.

"We got mixed up with some hard-case British soldiers on the train to York where we were supposed to change trains to Durham. When we arrived at York we must have dozed off because the next station we arrived at was in Edinburgh."

After their leave, it was back to camp and with winter approaching, Harry's troop was shifted to Westwell in Oxfordshire, a small village with a pub called The Wheel Inn, where the Kiwi soldiers had many enjoyable sessions. By this stage a German attack on Britain was imminent.

"I'm sure we thought we could defeat the German Army on our own. We sure had a lot to learn."

Soon after, the New Zealand troops were swimming in the sea while on manoeuvre at the British coast, when a German pilot in a low-flying Messerschmitt aircraft started to 'strafe' them, firing at them with automatic weapons.

"It wasn't a nice thing to do and was our first experience of anything like that. Nobody was hurt and we learned a good lesson."

The Battle of Britain, the air campaign waged by the German Luftwaffe against the United Kingdom during the summer and autumn of 1940 was soon in full swing. It was the first major campaign of the war to be fought entirely by air forces. The British RAF bravely prevented Germany from gaining air superiority during the battle, forcing Hitler to postpone and eventually cancel a subsequent invasion of Britain. Harry says the Kiwis witnessed some 'terrific' acrobatics during these battles.

"Those RAF pilots sure did a great job."

Towards the end of 1940, Harry's regiment was shifted back to the Farnham area in Surrey, where they were stationed at Swanthorpe Farm. Harry, Jeff 'Lofty' King and Keith Thompson volunteered to do a bit of farm work, which he said was much better than rifle drill on a cold frosty morning.

"Swanthorpe was a lovely place to camp. We had Christmas dinner there in 1940. The cooks put on an excellent meal and the army even turned on a rum ration. That was the last function we had in England as we were told to pack up for another shift."

Harry's regiment was told it was being deployed to Egypt. He travelled as part of an advance party to Newport on an unheated train, with the bad cold he had picked up before leaving Swanthorpe rapidly advancing to pneumonia. Harry was so ill, he had to be carried onto the ship on a stretcher, and was unconscious for 10 of the days they spent at sea.

On 5th March 1941, the Div Cav regiment was reunited in Egypt, where they spent a short time, before moving on to Greece.

"I travelled with the vehicles on a Liberty ship called the *Anglo Canadian*. We had travelled in more comfortable accommodation, but there was a war on after all. About halfway across the Mediterranean we were met by dive-bombing Stuka aircraft. It was the first time we had been bombed at sea and was not very nice. However we had Bren guns on tripods and managed to keep them from sinking us."

Once ashore at Piraeus Port, the Kiwis loaded their armoured vehicles onto trains to save wear and tear on the journey to Katerini.

They arrived on 4th April and that evening received the news that Number One and Number Two troops were to go forward to meet up with the British Armoured Division at Edhessa.

"I had a funny feeling in my stomach. We were on our way to meet the enemy. I still reckon I was scared."

Harry's intuition proved correct, and he was part of the first unit of 2nd New Zealand Division troops to engage with the enemy. The Kiwis took off from Edhessa and met up with British Brigadier Harold Charrington. Harry became part of a small Div Cav unit whose task it was to escort some British engineers across the northern border of Greece into Yugoslavia. The engineers were on a bridge-destroying mission in a bid to slow down the advancing German troops. It was dangerous work as the group came under intense fire.

"They had no fast vehicles and our three armoured cars filled the gap," said Harry.

The crew headed towards Bitolj where there was a bridge to be destroyed. All went well until the German forces came over a rise in the road. Lieutenant Darcy Cole managed to direct the engineers' explosive-laden lorry to turn around, as Lofty King bravely advanced and fired aggressively at the Germans. The Kiwis and the engineers they were protecting were able to retreat under enemy fire, stopping to set fire to two wooden bridges on the way.

"The Germans watched us from the surrounding hills but only fired small arm bullets at us. All our cars were hit but there were no casualties."

After they set the second bridge alight, the Kiwi troops continued to retreat towards the southern beaches of Greece, only to find they had been cut off at a culvert by a patrol of Germans.

"Lofty's car was in the lead and he attacked with both guns firing. Our two cars helped and the enemy retreated. They had about thirty vehicles against us but no tanks thank goodness."

Harry's crew managed to reconnect with the rest of the armoured brigade and then drove through the night over the perilous Veria Pass. "I took over the driving at about eleven o'clock at night and the boys lifted me out of the seat at eight the next morning, completely exhausted. The road was full of refugees and the drop over the side was several hundred feet. There was also a complete blackout. It was rough."

As the troop's chief mechanic, Harry did some running repairs on Darcy Cole's armoured car, which had made it over the pass with just one nut left holding the wheel in place.

With darkness a necessity to protect their position, the work had to be completed by torchlight under a tarpaulin. Harry also managed to fit a new half axle and brake drum on his own car, before continuing on with a new crew, driver Pat Gratton, gunner Shorty Ward and commander Bill Sutherland.

They travelled alone, as the other crews had already departed while Harry was doing the repairs. Harry, Pat, Shorty and Bill made it to Athens where they ditched the car and boarded a train to Corinth. They were strafed by the Luftwaffe all the way but managed to get there safely. After hitching a ride to Argos they headed straight for the aerodrome and found themselves in the firing line of some German planes, which started to shoot up the Hurricanes parked on the tarmac.

"Shorty and Pat hid under a truck and Bill and I took off. Unfortunately the truck was destroyed by German fire. Pat was killed and Shorty was badly wounded. I managed to drag him away and dress his wounds, which included a badly injured arm. A truck arrived and we loaded Shorty onto it. Bill thought it would be wise if I took Shorty to the hospital in Argos while he stayed and kept contact with the unit we were travelling with. He said I should go to the beach and find them later. It was a horrible mistake as it turned out."

Harry managed to get Shorty to the hospital, and was met by its sole doctor. He couldn't speak a word of English but immediately enlisted Harry as his 'theatre sister' to help him perform three amputations on wounded soldiers without any anaesthetic. It was a harrowing task.

"We couldn't communicate by talking, but he showed me what to do. I did my best. It was fortunate I'd done a bit of work with cattle at home but it wasn't a funny thing."

Later the horror of the day's events saw the doctor lose his nerve and he locked himself in his house, refusing to come out, leaving Harry in charge of the hospital.

"Here I was, with a hospital to run and no medical knowledge apart from how to fix a broken leg," said Harry. He muddled through with the help of an old midwife, some young girls and a 17 year old local boy named Jimmy, who was a 'terrific help'.

Unfortunately the three amputees all died, and in keeping with Greek custom, Harry attended one of the funerals. It was the first time he had been to a service at a Greek Orthodox church. Back at the hospital there was plenty of work to do and still no sign of the doctor. An exhausted Harry worked until about midnight when the local girls at the hospital made him up a bed on a stretcher.

"I had only been asleep for an hour when three journalists arrived. One of them was wounded. I got out of bed and took one of them, an American named Robert St John down to the beach on a motorbike to try and find a doctor. He was a tall chap and had to sit on the parcel-carrier on the back."

At the beach Harry managed to find two Australian doctors who were too busy to go straight to the hospital but promised to send an ambulance the next day. True to their word two ambulances arrived the following day and managed to clean the hospital out of most of the walking wounded. Soon after they left, the Germans started to advance and bomb the town.

"They didn't hit the hospital but there was a broken down ambulance nearby with a gas bottle sticking out. When it exploded it was worse than the bombs, blowing all the windows out."

With the help of a priest, Harry and Jimmy, the young Greek boy, managed to help the remaining few patients downstairs to the cellar. An English military policeman Harry knew arrived at the hospital to tell him the enemy was approaching fast, and would be in the town within half an hour.

"I hated to leave Shorty but the last thing I wanted to be was a prisoner- of-war. We had a talk and I said goodbye to him and the other chaps I had looked after. With a heavy heart, I walked up the steps from the cellar."

As he left the hospital, an officer and best friend of one of the men Harry had cared for, told him not to worry, that he would look after Shorty and the others, and he knew of a doctor nearby who could help. Harry headed straight for the wharf and managed to talk his way onto the HMS *Calcutta*, an anti-aircraft destroyer, which was being loaded with troops.

"I must have looked awful and at the end of my tether, as a sailor gave me a lovely cup of cocoa," he said.

They sailed shortly afterwards and it wasn't long before the ship was being attacked from the air. Harry lay on the deck beneath a three- point-seven anti-aircraft gun.

"A big sailor was pushing shells through a chute to the gun, and had the misfortune of getting his finger jammed in the chute which cut it clean off. He couldn't carry on so I took his place. Five hours and three hundred shells later, we arrived at Crete. The date was 26 April 1941, the day after Anzac Day. I'll never forget it."

Later, Harry heard the war correspondents had also managed to find their way out of Argos. Unbeknown to him, Robert St John, who he had taken to the beach in search of a doctor, was a famed globetrotting reporter, who mentioned their meeting in his 1942 book *Land of the Silent People*. Harry didn't hear about the book until he was in his nineties.

The HMS *Calcutta*, on which Harry made his spectacular escape, was sunk on its next voyage.

After arriving in Crete, Harry met up with a few of the boys from his regiment and was devastated to hear his good friends, Allan Risk and Lofty King, had been killed after being hit by an enemy Stuka attack. Harry also learned his regiment had been the first Imperial force to meet the Germans. Lofty was the first man to win a military medal in the campaign, which was awarded posthumously.

A few days after Harry's arrival in Crete, he was summonsed to a tent hospital, which had been established nearby.

"Imagine my surprise when I was taken to see Shorty. His arm had been removed but he had been cleaned up. The doctor asked me if I had put the dressings on Shorty in Argos, and I told him there had been nothing to change them with'. He said Shorty had been lucky, as the maggots in his wounds had kept them clean and saved his life."

Shorty was also a veteran of World War I, and was aged over 40 by this stage. He told Harry the week in Greece was worse than the three years he had spent fighting in France as a young man. Shorty was eventually sent home on a hospital ship, and Harry saw him once more, 24 years later in Hamilton, New Zealand.

"His experience was a great help to us in Greece. I remember the tin of Riverhead Gold tobacco he carried, and how the cigarettes he shared helped to soothe our nerves during the Greek campaign."

Gradually more Kiwis arrived at Crete.

"It was a lovely island. We had quite a good spell for a while. Food was short. However there were plenty of oranges, which of course we borrowed."

After the experiences of the British and Allied forces in mainland Greece, the uneasy peace after their retreat to Crete was welcomed. But it wasn't to last. The British had cracked some German codes and knew an invasion of the island was imminent. At the time, there were up to 28,000 troops on Crete to defend it under the command of New Zealand Major General Bernard Freyberg. Most were only lightly armed, as heavier equipment had been left in Greece during the evacuation. The Allied forces on the island endured air attacks for about a week before the morning of 20 May 1941, when the German invasion began in earnest.

Harry and fellow soldier, Arthur Collins, had eaten their breakfast of a few broken biscuits mixed up like porridge, before being sent to man a Bren gun on the summit of a nearby hill. It was from this vantage point they saw a terrifying spectacle, as the Germans launched their airborne invasion and the sky filled with parachutes.

The 12-day Battle of Crete was one of the most intense and dramatic of the Second World War, during which the Cretan people fought bravely alongside the Allied forces to protect their island. It was the first battle in which German paratroopers were used on a massive scale. Thousands of German paratroopers and glider-borne troops led the invasion, and suffered heavy casualties on the first day of fighting. However they managed to capture Maleme Airfield in western Crete the following day. This would prove a pivotal blow to the Allies and those defending the island, as the Germans were then able to fly in reinforcements in great numbers.

In the early days of the battle, Harry and the Div Cav troops were forced back towards the village of Galatas. The Germans had already gained possession of the prison at Agyha in the valley below.

The Kiwis settled into slit trenches near Pink Hill, by a road that led to the prison.

"We were in the way of some paratroopers who tried to take Galatas. We had some interesting battles but managed to hold our positions," said Harry.

The New Zealanders' stubborn defence of Pink Hill was an important feature of the fighting, as it took some wind out of the German advance. Harry's job as a runner, was to deliver messages between the troop and headquarters, which was located at the end of a drain.

"We had little communications established, so manpower was the most reliable source. I'll never forget taking a message to Major John Russell early one morning and he asked if I had had any breakfast. I said no, and he shared the little he had with me. That was the sort of chap he was."

Major Russell was the son of Major General Sir Andrew Hamilton Russell, of Gallipoli fame. He was later killed in action during the Western Desert campaign.

The Germans continued to advance slowly towards Galatas, reinforced with fresh troops who had landed at Maleme. On another message run, Harry stopped for a brief chat with Sergeant Jack Van Asch, before carrying on to headquarters.

"I had just arrived when all hell let loose. Aircraft bombed the hell out of us and the Major said to get into his slit trench with him until things quietened down. I was keen to get back to our troop and on my way, when I passed where Jack and I had talked, I saw he had been killed."

The relentless attack on the units defending Galatas ultimately forced the New Zealanders back, and the Germans captured the village. A brave and determined counter-attack by the New Zealand troops saw them retake Galatas that night. However the reoccupation would prove to be short lived. The Kiwis didn't have the men, artillery or air support to hold the village and the troops were exhausted. The decision was made to withdraw.

"We were quite disappointed when we had to vacate our position. However the unit on our flank had been overrun and we would have been cut off," said Harry.

The Allied troops were being forced back towards Canea when several New Zealand and Australian battalions took up positions along 42nd Street to provide a rear-guard for the retreating troops. The olive tree lined, unsealed road which ran from Hania to Tsikalaria, was nicknamed after the 42nd Field Company of the Royal Engineers.

When around 400 German troops were seen approaching 42nd Street, two Australian companies from the 2/7th Battalion charged with bayonets and small arms, followed by the 28th Māori Battalion and other New Zealand battalions.

"We arrived back in time to help with a bayonet charge on 42nd Street, however not many of us had bayonets so the only thing to do was shoot. The Māori Battalion was mixed up with this attack and I think the Germans were really frightened as they retreated."

This determined rear-guard action pushed the Germans back over 1600 yards, which gave the Allied troops vital time to get away.

With the battle to save the island all but lost, and vast numbers of German troops arriving, the British High Command authorised an evacuation to Sfakia in southwest Crete, where Allied troops could be removed from the island by the Royal Navy.

"We walked for something like 40 miles over the mountain to Sfakia. At this stage we were all tired out. How we made that trip, I will never know. I think it was fear. They put a good road over there after the

Signpost of the infamous
42nd Street.

war. I drove over it several times, on two occasions with a friend, the late Dudley Bell. He thought the same as I did, that it was one of the hardest things we ever had to do."

After they arrived at Sfakia, volunteers were called to go back up a hill and fight a rear-guard.

"All our gang went. But as it happened there was nothing to do, because the enemy was as tired as us."

Harry was sitting on a hill when Lieutenant Ian Bonifant passed him on the way to see General Freyberg, whose headquarters were in a cave lower down.

"He asked me to go with him and there was a lovely stream not far away. I bathed my aching feet in it while Ian was busy with the General. When he returned, he told me we had to pull out, so I suggested I go up and tell the chaps while he stayed and bathed his feet too. They were bleeding, as his boots had almost no soles left. He told me he had never asked anyone to carry his gear before. I convinced him I could manage if he looked after my rifle and kit bag. I think it was the only argument I ever won with him."

That evening the Kiwi troops arrived at the beach and were given a drink of tea. While they were waiting for the *Abdeil*, the mine laying ship, which would ferry them to Alexandria, Egypt, 'Bonny' suggested the men have a shave.

"I had a safety razor and we all used it. Boy it was blunt when the last bloke finished, but we felt clean."

Most of the men slept for a good part of the journey on the ship, and were given a bottle of beer each as they neared the port of Alexandria. "A friend, Ernie Read and myself thought we would drink Cairo dry of beer when we arrived. But all we could manage was a bottle between us on the ship. We gave the other one to a chap who needed it more," said Harry.

Although the battle for Crete was lost, the New Zealanders had fought with tenacity and courage in the face of overwhelming odds, with many acts of bravery and gallantry.

Lieutenant Ian Bonifant (left) with Colonel Clive
Pleasants of the 18th Battalion (New Zealand)
which also fought at Crete.

By its end, 671 New Zealand soldiers were killed, 967 wounded
and 2180 taken as prisoners-of-war.

During the battle, New Zealander Charles Upham was awarded
the first of two Victoria Crosses he would receive for his bravery and
wartime exploits.

Many of Harry's good friends were laid to rest in the British
cemetery at Crete. He visited the island six times after the war to pay
his respects and to return to the long silent battlefields.

"The Germans lost many young men in the battle too, who were
buried in a massive, beautifully kept cemetery. What a waste of good
lives war causes. And what for?"

After their arrival back in Egypt, the Divisional Cavalry spent
several months re-equipping.

Harry was among several Kiwis sent on a tank course, and while
he was there, managed to contract hepatitis.

"I was in hospital for six weeks which was almost a good rest."

New Zealand Club, Cairo, Egypt

On the last day of his stay, he received a letter from his old roop leader Darcy Cole, saying a place was open in his troop, with things warming up for the next desert battle.

Harry was keen, but his doctor had other ideas and he was despatched to Chevalier Island instead to look after a camp where hospital patients were sent to dodge the Italian's regular bombings.

"Our job was to put on a light meal, arrange entertainment for the patients, and keep the camp tidy. We played two-up as long as the officer-in-charge of the camp wasn't looking. One evening he caught us and wanted to know how it was played. Ossie James explained the rules, and on routine orders, the next morning the game was made legal with a limit of twenty piastres. Impossible. But he was covered."

Harry was on the island for eight weeks.

"We had a great holiday and became very fit. Every day, a friend, Gordon, and I swam out to King Farouk's yacht, which was anchored in Lake Timsah. Gordon knew the caretakers and we became very friendly."

The men were not allowed on board but would sit on a raft tied alongside and the caretakers on the yacht would pass lemonade down to them.

Harry (centre) enjoying leave with Norm Waters and Colin Miller, 1942.

Soon after Harry's return to Maadi Camp, near Cairo, he was posted to the desert with thousands of other New Zealand, British and Empire troops to fight in the Western Desert Campaign, known as the 'Desert War'.

Harry and eight other men were ordered to pick up nine armoured cars and deliver them to a British unit, a drive of about three hundred miles away.

The British were attached to 'Jock Columns', which were small combined groups of armoured cars, artillery and motorised infantry used in the North Africa campaign by the British Army's Western Desert Force, to harass the Italian forces.

After the Marmon-Herrington armoured cars were safely delivered, Harry was asked to drive five miles out from the base to pick up some soldiers, three Londoners, Corporal Ken Lee, Bill Benham and Fred Belch.

The men were engineers tasked mainly with finding wells and testing them.

They asked Harry to be their driver, and negotiate their armoured car over the tough country they had to work in.

"It was easy to miss a well, especially when you only had a sun compass. But Ken was a remarkable navigator and amazing tracker. I don't remember him ever missing one. He was among the finest soldiers I met during the war," said Harry.

A lot of this work went on over three day stints, which created some problems when it came to food.

"The Poms had no idea about rationing. We received rations

every day but if you went on a three day job you were given no extra, so had to do a bit of scrounging."

One day as the men were heading to a new job they came across a German ration truck stopped on the side of the road. The driver was tending to his wounded passenger.

"We took them prisoner and went back to the dressing station. They took the passenger but wouldn't take the German driver, so he ended up coming with us for the three days instead. He was a good cook and we had plenty of rations, including hermetically sealed bread, which we hadn't seen before. It kept fresh for weeks. Most of the tinned meat was horse meat but it was better than nothing."

The German driver's name was Christal, and he slept between Harry and Ken at night.

"He would wake one of us if he needed to get up. He was only nineteen and a farmer's son, and not interested in war at all. When we arrived back to our unit, they sent four big military policemen to take him prisoner. We had to laugh. It looked so silly."

Harry (left) with Londoners, Fred Belch, Bill Benham and Corporal Ken Lee.

Harry was with the Jock Columns for around three months and spent Christmas with the men at Agedabia.

"All we had for Christmas dinner was a muscle-bound fowl, which we had swapped with a Bedouin for some of our second hand tea. This was tea dregs, which we had dried out to use for bartering, or selling to tribespeople as real tea. Boy was that fowl tough."

The officer-in-charge, Major Catt, called the men over to his truck for a cup of tea and suggested they try and get through to Benghazi, as they had the only armoured vehicle in the column.

"While we were drinking our tea a message came through that the German 90th Light Infantry Division was between us and Benghazi so our little journey was called off. Thank goodness."

Soon after, Harry's crew was relieved by another British division, so they headed back to Cairo, arriving at the headquarters of the Jock Columns. Harry was not happy to be put on guard duty the first couple of nights, which he made clear to the British Sergeant Major.

"We didn't see eye to eye on that subject. I used his phone to ring Bonny and he was there within an hour in a staff car to pick me up. The only thing Bonny went crook about was my battle dress. I had swapped Ken for his English one and Bonny made me go straight to the quartermaster's store at Maadi to get another New Zealand one."

It wasn't long before Harry's troop was on the move again. This time it was to Syria, where they were to regroup, train, improve their defences, and protect the region, which was a potential route for German troops to capture the oil fields of the Middle East. The New Zealanders destination was a strategically located village called Djedeide with a population of about fifteen hundred people.

"The first night we slept among some big tents which hadn't been erected, and woke in the morning to find one had been flogged by the locals. The next night we set a trap and caught a donkey, which had another big tent loaded onto it. The local police eventually caught the thieves but we never got the tent back. A few weeks later we saw some children from the village wearing dresses and trousers made out of our tent material."

Despite this less than savoury introduction, Harry said the troops got on fairly well with the locals and once a night curfew was lifted they would regularly visit the villagers' homes.

Harry took this photograph of Syrian men with their goat.

"They had very clean homes, with dirt floors covered by lovely Persian carpets. The meal was usually goat meat stew, which was placed in a container in the centre of the room. Everyone would wash their hands and the guests would get the first dip. No spoons, just your hands. We were told not to refuse the local peoples' hospitality. The Popa would stand back and say, 'eat up, eat up'."

Harry was given a book about Syria by Divisional Cavalry Padre Harry Taylor, which mentioned that bears lived in the nearby hills.

"I told our troop leader, Harold Laing, and he asked Bonny if we could have a truck to drive into the hills to try and shoot one. But a job had to be done, so we missed out."

While's Harry's troop was at Djedeide, an order came through for a contingent to go to Cairo to pick up extra vehicles for the division. Harry was one of the men who went, and on his arrival was issued with a Bedford water truck with five hundred gallons of water aboard. Instead of going back to Syria, the contingent was told to turn up the desert road and had travelled quite some distance when a staff car drew up alongside the truck.

"Lieutenant Colonel Arthur Nicoll called out to me to follow him. He turned off the road and when we stopped I could see he had shot a gazelle. His driver used some of our water to cook it. This was the first fresh meat we had consumed for some time and it acted like a dose of salts."

Soon after, the Kiwis learned the British Eighth Army was in full retreat, after the Germans had decisively won the Battle of Gazala and captured Tobruk. By this stage, the German and Italian forces, commanded by the 'Desert Fox', Field Marshal Erwin Rommel, were striking deep into Egypt and threatening the British Empire's control of the Suez Canal and Palestine.

The New Zealand Division hurriedly returned from Syria and was sent to Mersa Matruh, an Egyptian resort town, west of Alexandria. On the way, they encountered thousands of British vehicles pouring eastwards.

"When we met up at Mersa Matruh, another soldier and myself were sent to patrol a small beach in case there was a sea landing. We were only armed with a .38 revolver each, so our task was impossible in any case. Nothing happened apart from some planes dropping a few bombs on the town."

Later, while patrolling the coastline, Harry and his crew spotted several Bren gun carriers on railway tracks at El Dabaa, a seaside town on the road to Alexandria. They 'acquired' the carriers, filling them with as much petrol as they could, and headed back to Marsa Matruh. On the way, they stopped at a nearby supply dump, which was about to be blown up, where Paddy Flynn, a good mate of Harry's, found several cartons of American beer. These were quickly commandeered by the Kiwis and loaded into the carriers.

Rather than remain in a defensive position at Mersa Matruh, General Bernard 'Tiny' Freyberg moved his New Zealand Division further south into the desert area of Minqar Qaim, where it could play a more mobile role.

However within days, the New Zealanders had been completely cut off from the Allied forces to the east by the advancing Germans.

Their only chance was to force their way through a gap in the ring of Germans surrounding them. The breakout came during the early hours of 28 June 1942, when members of the New Zealand Division, led by the 4th Brigade, burst through enemy lines, using hand-to-hand combat to savage effect.

As the battle unfolded, the majority of the Division was able to slip though a gap further south, and retreat to the Alamein Line.

This incredible event in New Zealand military history was led by Brigadier Lindsay Inglis, as General Freyberg had been wounded and was recuperating in Cairo.

By this stage, the Germans had had another victory over the Eighth Army at Mersa Matruh, and there were real concerns they might break the Alamein Line. However the Allied forces were finally able to hold their position and repel the German advance during the First Battle of El Alamein, which raged throughout July 1942.

When the fighting eventually reached a stalemate, Rommel dug in to give his troops time to regroup. General Auchinleck, Commander in Chief of the Allied forces, ceased offensive operations on 31 July, to strengthen the Eighth Army's defences ready for the next counter-offensive by the Axis troops. Both sides were exhausted.

Even in the heat of battle, there was still time for some of life's 'ordinary' moments, with Harry and two fellow soldiers celebrating their birthdays in July.

"Harry Drury had some brandy, which we were going to use to celebrate, but then his carrier was shot up. There was no loss of life, but our brandy was destroyed. We joked that Harry had already drunk it and that's why he lost his carrier."

When things quietened down at the end of the First Battle of El Alamein, Harry's troop was given four days leave in Cairo.

"Instead of going to Maadi, a few of us jumped off the truck at Mena and booked into a pension owned by an old Greek man, who we called Uncle. The first thing he did was take our pistols off us and put them in a safe. He was a great old chap. He also kept our money safe and only allowed us to have so much each day. Some other chaps came in from the camp and Uncle found extra beds and put them up. We had a delightful leave and almost felt like having another go at Rommel at the end of it."

In early August, British Prime Minister Winston Churchill and General Alan Brooke, the British Chief of the Imperial General Staff, decided to appoint XIII Corps commander William Gott to the Eighth Army command, replacing General Auchinleck. However Gott was killed before taking command when the transport plane he was travelling in was shot down. On 13 August, Lieutenant-General Bernard Montgomery became Eighth Army commander instead, a man Harry described as a 'breath of fresh air'.

Rommel's anticipated attack came at the end of August 1942, but would be repulsed within a week by the Allies in the Battle of Alam el Halfa. Harry said a plague of flies and basket bombs were two things he would never forget about this battle. His troop's job was to coax enemy tanks through a gap where they would be fired on by Allied guns.

"The ruse worked perfectly and many German tanks were destroyed."

It was about this time Harry's unit learned one of its most respected officers, Major John Russell, had been killed.

"He stepped on a mine which was most unfortunate. He was a fine soldier, and the unit missed him. I was privileged to become friendly with his son John after the war, who sadly never knew his father."

Harry said after the battle was over and Rommel was repulsed, the Allied troops felt the tide was turning.

"We were taken out of the firing line and camped near a lovely beach where we could swim in reasonable safety. We still had our tanks and treated them as home. Around this time General Montgomery came and addressed us, which filled us with confidence."

Harry said his crew's earlier confiscation of the Bren gun carriers proved fortuitous at El Alamein, where they were put to good use patrolling the area south of the town near the Qattara Depression.

"We had different crews and used the twelve carriers virtually non- stop. It was all bluff, as we only had rifles, and no machine guns for armament. Our job was to kid the German patrols into some sand dunes where the anti-tank boys were hidden and would open fire. It worked and the Germans never tried an attack on that area."

Harry said around this time, two tanks from his division, including his own, were blown up in a minefield.

"Our tank only had one track blown, but the other tank had two. Because I was troop mechanic and had some cunning pieces of gear stored on board, I thought it was possible to save our tank. My commander, Sergeant Jack Riddell, said he would help me, but our new troop leader wasn't too keen on the idea. He gave in in the end, but insisted a radio operator stayed behind too, so we could maintain contact. Joff Kay volunteered and all was going well until the Germans saw what we were doing and gave us a hurry up."

The men hid behind the tank, and when danger passed, Jack Riddell decided to have a brew up, said Harry.

"He climbed into the tank to get a tin of coffee and milk, which had come in a parcel from home, then jumped back down onto the ground."

By this stage, some British engineers had arrived to clear mines in the area. Incredibly, they identified a mine right between Jack's boot marks, which were still on the ground where he had landed.

"We were lucky not to have all been blown to pieces."

Once the running repairs to the tank were completed, Harry, Jack and Joff drove back to Squadron Headquarters.

Harry and Jack were put into another tank, and a few days later, were back on patrol when a bomb landed about twenty yards in front of them and exploded.

This time, Jack's luck ran out.

"I was in the driver's seat and Jack fell down behind me with blood all over his chest. I tore his shirt open but there were no wounds. He said it was his head, and then the penny dropped. Jack had stopped a piece of shrapnel and half his head was missing. Some stretcher bearers came over and I had the task of lifting my old friend down onto the stretcher."

Harry and radio operator Derek Tatton drove the tank back to headquarters, smoking many cigarettes on the way.

Jack Riddell (left) with Jim Neilson (right) and an
Arab man.

"When we arrived back, I was put in another tank and sent on a mission. Tat was told to clean the tank out. He told me afterwards it was the hardest job he ever had to do, and I quite believed him. Jack was a special person. We couldn't even attend his burial service conducted by Padre Harry Taylor, as we were too busy on patrol."

With the Axis forces just 66 miles from Alexandria, and close to other major population centres as well as the Suez Canal, the Allied forces couldn't allow the status quo to remain. It took the Second Battle of El Alamein to drive the enemy out of Egypt for good. By the time the Eighth Army was ready to strike in October 1942, it had established a significant intelligence advantage over Rommel's forces. This had also allowed the Royal Navy and to a lesser extent, the Desert Air Force, to destroy many of the enemy's supply ships destined for North Africa, considerably reducing its fuel and ammunition supply. The Eighth Army had by this time, built up a much larger force of nearly 200,000 men (made up of 10 divisions and several independent brigades) compared to 116,000 Axis troops.

With the Second Battle of El Alamein in the offing, Harry's unit was dispatched to El Hamman on 19 October 1942. As always, General Freyberg wanted to fight the battle from the front. His team removed the main gun out of his tank and replaced it with a dummy barrel to allow room for a radio set, and to ensure extra crew could fit inside in reasonable comfort.

"The General's driver was a chap named George Nicholls. He was a good choice as George was a character and he and Tiny were the best of friends. It was funny to see them pacing up and down and talking together in the evenings when things hadn't been going very well. George never once told us what they had discussed."

Harry ready for action in the Western Desert.

Harry's Number One troop from C Squadron Divisional Cavalry was then detailed to act as a protective force, with his newly issued Stuart tank one of five vehicles to accompany General Freyberg throughout the desert campaign.

The protective troop always travelled in desert formation, with the navigator, Bruce Jones's tank in the lead followed by the General. There was one tank on the left, usually two or three chains apart, and Harry's tank on the right. The General was known to set a rollicking pace with the others expected to keep up.

"It wasn't a job we wanted but it turned out to be very entertaining. The General came and gave us a talk about what our position entailed. He mentioned that saluting was not on the menu because there would be officers around most of the time. But if a high ranking officer arrived, we were to at least stand up."

The Second Battle of El Alamein started on 23rd October with the New Zealand Division playing a key role. Its initial task was to break in through the enemy defences, which were covered by deep minefields. On the first day of the battle Harry's unit was sent as far forward as was reasonably safe and listened to the noise of shells passing overhead for three hours or more.

"It was hard to describe how it affected you. Personally I felt quite numb," said Harry.

After a few hours the New Zealand infantry started to march through, and as their old troop leader Ian 'Bonny' Bonifant passed close by, Harry and his friends asked how his flat feet were standing up to all the walking.

"He was quite rude and called us cheeky bastards. By this time he had been promoted to Colonel of the 25th Infantry Battalion. He told me afterwards he was nervous, as he didn't know the men and they didn't know him. But he proved himself to be an exceptional leader."

In the early hours of the following morning, General Freyberg arrived, and Harry's troop proceeded through the cleared minefields led by Sergeant Bruce Jones, who was a 'terrific navigator', said Harry.

"We got through the minefields quite safely, but then of course it had to rain. The enemy had already gotten away on the good going, and our Division Headquarters became stuck in the boggy sand. Our tanks spent the rest of the day pulling the trucks out."

Troop leader Darcy Cole told Harry to 'V' two tanks together and a Lance Corporal named Laurie came and laid a bedroll between the tanks.

Harry had visions of sleeping in sheets that night but had to take one of the men to a dressing station to get a wound fixed and arrived back late. He rolled out his bedroll between the tanks and climbed in.

"About 3am a squeaky voice asked what the time was. I thought it was Laurie so told him to shut up, but it turned out to be General Freyberg who was sleeping between me, and the gunner Les Worsley. Later we reckoned those sleeping arrangements were so Les or I would stop any piece of stray shrapnel, rather than it hitting the General."

(Left to right) Derek Tatton (radio operator), Cliff Davis (gunner), and Harry Spencer (driver) on a Stuart tank at El Alamein, Egypt, 16 July 1942. Absent: Jack Riddell (commander). *Photograph taken by H Paton, Ref DA-02569-F. Courtesy of Alexander Turnbull Library, Wellington, New Zealand*

Harry said General Freyberg was a 'fantastic chap' to serve with. "Every now and again when it was quiet, we would sit out in the desert with him and have a bit of a yarn. He always called me by my Christian name and would ask me to do something rather than ordering me to do it. It was a relationship based on trust."

After the war, Harry went to three parties in Cairo where General and Lady Freyberg were also in attendance.

"Some of the old Colonels would be standing there all stiff to attention, and old Tiny and I would be having a yarn about the funny things that happened."

The battle continued, and as the Germans pulled back, the Allied forces followed as soon as possible. At their next stop, General Freyberg decided to load the tanks onto transporters to save wear and tear. The starter motor on Harry's tank burned out as he was loading it, so the General asked if he could ride a motorbike back to the workshops to get a replacement.

"The workshops were around 70 miles back, and the going was not very good. When I arrived, the boys made me a cup of tea while someone found a new starter motor. I decided to go back to the troop across the desert rather than using the road, which was cluttered up with traffic. The General got a surprise when I told him I'd come back through the desert, as he thought it was full of Germans. I didn't see any, and he seemed quite pleased about that. So was I. Our convoy was about to take off, and I was lucky they hadn't gone without me. I wouldn't have enjoyed riding that motorbike for another 300 miles."

With heavy losses of men and equipment, and a critical fuel shortage, it was apparent to Rommel by early November 1942 that the battle was lost. He began to plan the Axis troops' retreat. However Hitler ordered him to 'stand to the last'.

On 2 November, the Allied troops unleashed Operation Supercharge, with the objective of taking over the Axis forces' supply routes, reducing their fuel supply and causing the general disintegration of the enemy army. The New Zealand Division played a key role, breaking through the German positions and getting around Rommel's flank during what proved to be one of the most intense and destructive battles of the campaign. By 4 November, Rommel decided to defy Hitler's orders and withdraw west towards Libya in order to save the remainder of his force. All Axis troops had been withdrawn from Egypt by 11 November 1942 and the Second Battle of El Alamein was won.

The Allied victory over Rommel and his forces proved a significant turning point in the Western Desert campaign. It was their first decisive victory in a major offensive against the Axis forces since the start of the war and gave them a huge psychological boost. As Winston Churchill would later famously say, "Before Alamein we never had a victory. After Alamein we never had a defeat."

The Axis forces retreated to El Agheila where they entrenched, with the Allied forces on their tail. As Harry's troop made their way into Libya, they were surprised to come across a porcelain bath and two drums of water.

"We weren't in a hurry, so our troop all had a bath. It was lovely. The General had just got back from Cairo so he didn't indulge."

Harry's unit joined back up with the Divisional Cavalry and learned they were to take part in a 'left hook' or wide outflanking movement on the German position at El Agheila.

"This was a very secret move and I nearly blew it. My friend, Sergeant Snow Nicholas, was on the last shift as guard, so I kidded him to light my primus and make a brew. It was still dark and Snow lit his primus in his tank as we didn't want to show any lights. He grabbed my fuel bottle to pump it, but I didn't realise that earlier, I'd lost the washer off the filler cap when I was filling it up with high-octane petrol in the dark. A flame shot out and set a fire going inside Snow's tank. Thankfully Snow was a calm soldier. He started the fire extinguisher then sat on top of the turret until he was sure the fire was out. He told me I was a 'bloody fifth columnist' and a few other things. He was a bit short of hair after the incident but as he said afterwards, we still got our cup of tea. The General wouldn't have been very pleased if the tank had gone up in smoke. Snow saved the day for being so calm under stress. He and I remained very good friends for the rest of his life."

The New Zealand Division completed its 'left hook' but General Montgomery's offensive plans didn't come off as hoped, and the Axis troops were able to retreat to Nofilia, about 100 miles west of El Agheila.

There were some short-lived but fierce skirmishes once the Allied troops advanced on Nofilia, but the Eighth Army was unable to get to the rear of the withdrawing Axis forces. Rommel was able to withdraw again, this time to Buerat with the intention of retreating further to Tripoli and ultimately to Tunis, the capital of neighbouring Tunisia.

The New Zealand Division set up camp at Nofilia, where they spent Christmas 1942.

"The army did us proud with a delightful Christmas dinner and even some beer – something we hadn't seen for some time," said Harry.

They remained in reserve in the area until 15 January when General Freyberg joined the troops for the push towards Tripoli. This proved to be a bad day for Harry's regiment with a couple of casualties. Overnight the German rearguard left, and Harry's unit set a cracking pace in pursuit.

"The General said 'push on', and we did."

On the way they passed several broken down, mainly Italian, tanks.

"The General ran into three of these tanks and stopped to brew a cup of tea. We didn't see what was happening and carried on a short distance. Then I spotted an M13 Italian tank coming back to its mates, its gun swinging on to us. I pushed our gun towards their turret and was able to stop them. We were only about thirty yards away and travelling fairly fast so it was over in seconds. I hopped out and started pulling the prisoners out of the open door of their tank. My commander, Paddy Flynn, went crook later because I wasn't armed. Anyway it saved the day and we were pleased we didn't lose the General, and Brigadier Weir who was travelling with us too."

Some years later, Harry was marching with the Brigadier at an Anzac parade.

"He said, 'Haven't I met you before?' I said, 'Remember the day we got those Italian tanks?' His reply was, 'Were you with that bloody outfit?' He travelled with us quite often and was the commanding officer of the New Zealand Divisional Artillery. He was good at it too."

On the way to Tripoli, Harry's unit arrived at a wadi, or dry gully, where the enemy were cleaning their guns.

"We got the two bosses out of the danger area then ran into some Sherman tanks of the Greys, who were our Division's support regiment. They were a pretty sight. A tank battle started almost immediately with the Germans. Our General was sitting in his tank looking through his binoculars and thoroughly enjoying the view."

Paddy Flynn enjoying a bath in the desert.

Harry's commander, Paddy Flynn, had a bedroll on the front of their tank, which contained a new battle dress he had obtained by 'devious' means. A shell landed a bit short and a piece of shrapnel went straight through the bedroll. Paddy got out of the tank, took off the bedroll and discovered a big hole in his prized battle dress.

"He had a good vocabulary and with much waving of his arms told the Germans what he thought of them. This was in the middle of a fairly heavy barrage. We laughed about it afterwards. Paddy was a real character, a good soldier and friend."

Afterwards the General told his troops to 'push on' for most of the day. The trek to Tripoli was across some of the roughest country Harry's unit had encountered. Finally the city came into sight, which was a relief for all concerned.

General Freyberg confers with Brigadier Weir at Tripoli. *Photograph taken by H G Paton. Ref DA-02859-F. Courtesy of Alexander Turnbull Library, Wellington, New Zealand.*

The Axis forces had already withdrawn from Tripoli, which had been taken by the Eighth Army on 23 January 1943, cutting off Rommel's main supply base. Rommel switched his line of supply to Tunis instead and moved his troops to occupy an extensive set of defensive fortifications known as the Mareth Line, which had been constructed by the French between Medenine and Gabès in Southern Tunisia prior to World War II to repel an Italian attack from Libya. Rommel hoped the use of the Mareth Line would enable the Axis forces to block the Allies on their approach to Tunisia.

With the enemy already gone, the New Zealand troops were able to have some much-need respite in Tripoli.

"The General had pushed most of us, and himself, to the limit. Our vehicles were in need of maintenance and we needed a good break."

Harry said Tripoli wasn't very exciting but they still had plenty to do, working on their tanks and unloading ships. They came across three enormous vats of wine and managed to acquire plenty of it.

"We called it purple death and it was well named. While working on the ships we also managed to acquire some goodies like tinned fruit and some innocent looking boxes of sweets, which had a bottle of rum packed in the middle. It was apparently destined for some American tank crews and was very acceptable."

By this stage the troops of the New Zealand Division had already garnered a reputation for helping themselves to enemy, and even Allied, heavy weapons and transport and other goods, which led to the unit being nicknamed 'Freyberg's Forty Thousand Thieves'.

The General went to Cairo for a conference, and on his return lectured the Division about taking goods from the ships. That didn't stop him opening tins of fruit that evening and saying 'eat up boys', said Harry.

"He must have known they weren't on ration but he loved opening the tins. We had little parties and the pleasure of entertaining some of the Air Force chaps with the aid of purple death. I don't think they would have been safe to fly with the next day. When we visited them, we found they had even better grog. The break was wonderful for morale and I think we started to look forward to the next encounter with the enemy."

On 4 February 1943, a victory parade was organised at Tripoli, with a great collection of leaders in attendance such as British Prime Minister Winston Churchill, Chief of Imperial Staff Sir Alan Brooke, Generals Alexander, Montgomery, Freyberg, and others.

"It was a pleasure for us to be in the lead of the Division with the General's tank in first place, and it was a great sight to see Winston Churchill taking the salute from the reviewing stand. Our troop then took up a place by the stand and the General joined the VIPs. We certainly had a good seat."

On 2 March 1943, Harry's unit left Tripoli on the three-day journey to Medenine where the Eighth Army had forced the Axis troops.

On their arrival they helped to repulse another attack by Rommel at the Battle of Medenine, which would prove the Desert Fox's last offensive in North Africa. General Montgomery deployed large numbers of anti-tank guns in the path of the offensive.

After losing a staggering 52 tanks, Rommel called off the assault.

A couple of days later he returned to Germany to try and press Hitler to comprehend the reality of the Axis troops' dire situation in the desert. He wasn't successful and lost command of the forces to General Hans-Jurgen von Arnim. Rommel never returned to Africa.

Over 30 years later, Harry and his wife Madge were at a show in Stuttgart, Germany, when they got talking to an elderly German woman and her adult son.

"They turned out to be Rommel's widow, and his son Manfred who became Mayor of Stuttgart. They were very nice people and Manfred later wrote to me," said Harry.

One person he couldn't tell about this meeting was his friend, Captain Charles Upham, who won the Victoria Cross twice for his exploits at Crete and the First Battle of El Alamein.

"If Charlie had known I had corresponded with Rommel's son he would never have spoken to me again."

Harry remembers the last time he and Charles Upham got together.

"He said, 'You know Harry, we made a mistake at the end of the war, instead of making something of our lives we should have taken a country over'. We used to have a few funnies."

The New Zealand Division's tanks were transported about 200 miles to the Tebaga Gap, which continued to be strongly defended by the Germans. Harry's troop was stationed at Hill 201 where he received his only wound of the war, something he puts down to luck, and being able to 'duck fast'.

A lone enemy plane's rear gunner put a burst of explosive bullets into the turret of Harry's tank where Les Worsley was manning a Browning machine gun against the aircraft.

"Les fell down and as I was working on him, Paddy Flynn tore up and said, 'Les is okay, it's you who is bleeding'. A small piece of shrapnel had struck the lobe of my ear and blood was pouring out of it. I didn't feel anything and thought it was a bit of a joke. Les carried the shrapnel that hit him that day for the rest of his life."

The Eighth Army attacked that afternoon, and the next morning General Freyberg wanted to visit the British tank commander, Lieutenant Colonel Kellett, taking Harry's troop along with him.

"While he was talking to Lieutenant Colonel Kellett, who was standing inside his tank having a shave, a lone German plane flew over and dropped a bomb behind our tank. A piece of shrapnel flew past the General and the rest of us, and killed the Colonel. That was one more reason why I have always been a fatalist," said Harry.

On 21 March 1943, the reinforced Kiwi troops executed a left hook around the main Axis defences through the Tebaga Gap in southern Tunisia.

On 26 March Operation Supercharge II was launched, and within two days the main Axis forces on the Mareth Line had been forced to withdraw due to the flanking threat from the advancing British 1st Armoured and New Zealand Divisions.

This major blow dealt by the Allies led to the complete disintegration of the enemy resistance and Mareth position. General Montgomery sent a personal message to General Freyberg congratulating the New Zealand troops on their efforts. With the Battle of Tebaga Gap over, the Allies pushed on through terrain that was more fertile than they had seen for some time. The enemy still had to be cleared out, which wasn't easy, said Harry.

"We eventually arrived at a place called El Djem and our vehicles were in need of a good overhaul. A mechanic named Jack Heywood and myself were working on my tank when the General came over and told us to grab a jeep and go and have a look at the some ruins of an old Roman amphitheatre about five miles away. It was one of the Old Wonders of the World."

Jack acquired a vehicle and about five men, including Harry, went to have a look at the impressive Roman Amphitheatre of Thysdrus, which was built around 238AD and used mainly for gladiator shows and chariot races in its heyday. After sampling some local brew they had acquired in the village, Harry said the Kiwis were in the mood to play.

"At the ruins, Jack threw us to the lions or whatever it was they did back in those days. It was good fun."

On the way back to base they met some British army troops coming up the road in the opposite direction. An officer with a red band around his hat pulled out of the column a few chains ahead of the Kiwis' jeep and forced them into a ditch. Jack called the officer a 'Pommy bastard'. He must have heard, because a short time later, when the Kiwis had almost got the jeep back out of the ditch, he arrived back.

"The officer said, 'Did you call me a Pommy bastard?' Jack, who was a wrestler and as strong as a bull didn't back down, and said, 'Yes, because you put us in the ditch'. The officer said, 'Well, I've come back to tell you I was the third child in my family, and my mother and father were married before the first one arrived, so I'm no bastard."

The British officer turned out to be General Brian Horrocks, Commander of X Corps, which included the New Zealand Division. He was in the company of the Kiwis on several occasions after the incident, but never mentioned it again.

The New Zealand Division's next move was towards Enfidaville, about 60 miles south of Tunis.

"There was another battle looming, so General Freyberg decided to take only one tank forward to have a closer look at the terrain. He went in Bruce's tank and they stopped at the forward infantry to confer with the officer-in-charge. They were already in full view of Takrouna, a hill with a commanding view over miles of territory, however the General decided he would like an even closer look. He told Bruce to pull over behind a house with a sloping roof. He wanted to climb up to get a better view with the aid of his binoculars. The enemy saw this move and shelled them for a while."

General Freyberg told Bruce to radio Brigadier Weir to tell him he wanted him up there too.

"While they were waiting, he told the radio operator, Fred Brayfield, to pick some peas from a nearby garden. Fred wasn't keen as they were still being shelled, but he did it. Fred was my driver in Italy at a later date and was killed at Forli after I came home."

The General was still sitting on the front of the tank shelling and eating peas when he passed back through the infantry lines.

"The boys were calling out, 'Hi Tiny' and he was waving back at them."

While stationed at Enfidaville, Harry took a high-ranking German officer prisoner.

"I was walking back to the troop alone, after doing some reconnaissance with Bruce, and a German officer came out of some scrub and surrendered to me. I took his Luger pistol off him and stuck it in my belt alongside my .38 revolver. I wasn't very well dressed, wearing just a pair of shorts, beret and boots. My prisoner spoke English very well and kept quoting the Geneva Convention, saying he couldn't be disarmed by anyone of a lower rank than him. His mood changed when we walked up to General Freyberg's tank and I waved the General a salute and handed him the Luger. I never found out who the German was, but the General gave him a good dressing down because he had used all his ammunition before he surrendered, killing some of our men in the process."

This would be the last time Harry would see the General until they were back in Cairo, as Freyberg was posted to another temporary command. Brigadier Kippenberger took his place.

"Kip hated tanks so we didn't have much to do until one day Bruce's tank and ours answered the call to take the New Zealand Minister of Defence, Fred Jones, up to have a look at the front. He travelled in our tank for protection with me driving, and Fred in the seat behind me. We had a good old yarn on the way up. He had come over to tell us that some of the long serving men were to go home for leave which was good news."

Tunis finally fell to the Eighth Army on 7 May, which prompted the surrender of the remaining, exhausted Axis forces on 13 May 1943.

The war in North Africa was over with the exploits of the 2nd New Zealand Divisional Cavalry during this period 'under great leadership' going down in history, said Harry.

"We only managed to keep out of trouble by sheer cheek at times."

With the war in the desert won, the stage was now set for the start of the tough Italian campaign.

The New Zealand troops had to leave their faithful tanks behind and ride in trucks for the long journey back to Egypt.

They had a short stay in Benghazi, where the Division was given two bottles of beer per man, which had been packed in boxes of four dozen.

"Our troop leader was commissioned to collect the beer on behalf of the Division and being an enterprising type, acquired some extra grog for the 5th RMT, which didn't actually exist, as there was only a 4th and a 6th."

On their arrival back at Maadi, the New Zealanders were well treated and given leave. Harry, Ernie Read and Jim Galvin, travelled by train to Luxor to visit the Valley of the Kings.

"It was rather fascinating but very hot. It took quite a lot of beer to keep us going."

Back at Maadi, Harry was surprised to learn his name wasn't on the list of troops returning to New Zealand on leave. Neither was his good friend Snow Nicholas, who had also had a fairly rugged time and needed a rest.

Ernie Read, Harry, and Jim Galvin in Egypt.

"I was supposed to go home as a mechanic and help train the armoured brigade, but Colonel Bonifant rang and said, 'You're not going home, you're going to Italy'. I said, 'Thanks very much'. They wanted 40 Non- Commissioned Officers from the Division who'd had a lot of experience with armour and tanks to go to Italy and I was among them."

Harry lost his job as troop mechanic and was promoted to the ranks of Lance Corporal, Temporary Corporal and Acting Sergeant all at the same time.

He was sent on a course to study the new Staghound armoured cars.

"They were very modern machines sporting a 37mm gun and two Browning .30 calibre machine guns. Jimmy Barron and I were detailed to put them through a few tests. We found they had a few faults and condemned them for our use in Italy. I was still landed with one but would rather have had a jeep."

Among the 40 men selected to serve in the Div Cav alongside Harry in Italy, was a 22 year old associated registered accountant, Corporal Robert Muldoon, who completed his accountancy exams while serving overseas. He would later become New Zealand's 31st Prime Minister between 1975 and 1984.

The unit sailed for Italy on the *Letitia* (which was later renamed the *Captain Cook*) and after an uneventful voyage, arrived at the port of Taranto in southern Italy to be greeted by a mighty storm.

After the heat of the desert, the harsh wintry conditions in Italy were a shock for the New Zealanders. Once their vehicles arrived in early November 1943, the Division took off for pastures new.

"On the way we passed through many vineyards, some of which had been booby trapped. One of our chaps, Bert Jarman, had completed a mines course and he soon cleared the vines of mines, much to the pleasure of the locals who fed us lovely grapes."

The men eventually arrived at Lucera, not far from the explosive combat zone of the Sangro River, which the enemy had ideas of holding for the winter. Harry's troop was detailed to patrol up the river and got a surprise when an unusual looking aeroplane belly-landed nearby.

"We captured the crew and I sent a message to Major Nick Wilder. He told us to hold on to it with our lives as it was a Messerschmitt 210, the first one they had seen. The Major sent a raw recruit out in a jeep to collect the prisoners. In his excitement he rolled the jeep and broke the arm of one of the prisoners, who had landed without receiving a bruise."

The Messerschmitt 210 planes were German heavy fighter and ground attack aircraft. They were plagued with problems throughout the war, having design flaws, which caused poor flight characteristics. The 210 had only limited service in 1943 before it was replaced by its successor, the Messerschmitt 410 or 'Hornet'.

While doing their river patrols, Harry's unit left their Staghounds near three houses, which had booby trapped wine barrels inside.

"Bert soon fixed that, and the boys had a good party with the owners. When we arrived back, an Italian grabbed me and led me out to the riverside. In broken English he pointed out where all the enemy gun emplacements were. I plotted them and when we arrived back at camp, troop leader Jim Cooke showed them to Major Wilder who was more than pleased."

An attack was arranged for the next morning, with Major Wilder organising the anti-tanks to 'blast hell' out of those positions.

After the war, Wilder told Harry he would never know how many lives he had saved by listening to the Italian chap, who had previously tried to warn a Sergeant but was ignored.

The Div Cav unit was moved to Cupello, just south of the Sangro River valley on 12 November to cover the left flank of the New Zealand Division.

"Our troop was once again detailed to patrol forward and that was where I would have liked a jeep. My gunner Les Worsley and I had to walk on patrol as we couldn't get the cars off the road without getting stuck."

One day they met up with an Italian who spoke reasonably good English and seemed to be on the Allied side.

Harry took a chance and went with him to a small farm in the area, which was owned by one of the Italian man's friends.

"My crew ended up going to the farm every evening where we were made very welcome, given a meal and the best of wine to drink. I never let the boys swap names for obvious reasons. Fred my driver gave us all fictitious names, which ended with an 'O'. We would leave at 9pm if the Italian chaps didn't arrive with some information for us, but mostly they did, and it was stuff we couldn't get ourselves. Major Wilder's only complaint was that I didn't send the information sooner."

Harry said he found out years later the chap who helped them was from the Mafia.

"I had always suspected it, but never knew for sure until much later."

Harry said he was constantly cold, hungry and homesick in Italy, with the unrelenting horrors of war taking their toll.

One day, in freezing wintry conditions, he and some fellow soldiers couldn't find anywhere to sit to eat their food, so they lay the bodies of two frozen Italian soldiers on top of each other, threw a cover over them, and sat on them while eating their baked beans.

It was an action that would stay with Harry for the rest of his life.

"I never ate baked beans again, and if I ever saw them, I was taken right back to that moment in Italy," said Harry.

Late in 1943, Div Cav became involved in operations in Orsogna and Castel Frentano, towns in the Abruzzo region of Italy.

One day, two troops, including Harry's, were working on the road to Lanciano when they were halted by anti-tank gunfire. Les Worsley and Harry went for a walk among the trees and spotted the deadly German 88mm gun that had them covered.

"We were about level with Castel Frentano, a town still occupied by the enemy. One of the chaps from the other troop, Jim Logan, went to get help from some British Sherman tanks who were handy, but came back fuming when they refused to come to our aid. We were then recalled, but Les wanted to try our big gun out so I told him to have a go. When he started firing towards Castel Frentano the others did the same. Our infantry attacked the town and took it. Les always reckoned he was the one who shifted the enemy armour out of the town."

Just out of Castel Frentano were some old damaged brickworks, on a short road leading towards Orsogna, which was still in enemy hands. "The brickworks were at the start of the road known the 'Mad Mile' because it was under continuous fire. It was certainly an entertaining experience to travel on it."

One day, in December 1943, just after Harry had crossed the Mad Mile, he saw two of his old friends, Sandy Gibson and Bill Sutherland standing by a Sherman tank. As Harry shared a brew with his friends, he was unaware this would be their last time together in Italy. His war was about to end.

One evening soon after, troop leader Jim Logan called Harry over to his Staghound and said Colonel Bonifant wanted to talk with him.

'Flash Kiwis', Harry (right) and Bill Holland about to represent the Divisional Cavalry at the wedding of Captain Godfrey 'Harry' Stace, to a New Zealand Army nursing sister in Egypt. Bill was later killed in action in Italy. Pictured right, is Bill's grave.

The badly damaged brickworks, near Castel Frentano, Italy, at the start of the 'Mad Mile'. *Photograph taken by George Kay. Ref DA-06245-F. Courtesy of Alexander Turnbull Library, Wellington, New Zealand.*

"The talk was all in code, with Bonny indicating I had to be ready to go home to New Zealand at six o'clock the next morning. I told him to forget it. His answer was, 'You will do as you are bloody well told Spencer', which obviously wasn't in code."

Just like that, Harry learned that after almost four years of hard toil, blood, sweat, and dodging bullets, bombs and mines, his war was over. During the harsh winter campaign in Italy, reinforcements were steadily replacing brave men like Harry who had fought relentlessly through battle after difficult battle with very little rest or respite.

That night, the men in Harry's troop took up a collection and presented it to him.

"I didn't want to take it but they insisted. You wouldn't have met a better gang of chaps. All but one of the 40 of us who went to Italy was still alive at that stage."

Sadly, Harry's old crew were all later killed at Forli. Many years later he was in a touring party, which stopped at the town for lunch.

He wanted to visit the men's graves but was told they had been shifted to Cassino. Harry found out later the graves hadn't been moved at all, so was sad to have missed the opportunity to pay his respects to those lost mates.

Harry left his troop the next morning, as he was told. It was the last he would see of Colonel Ian Bonifant for some time. Bonny ended the war as a Brigadier and he and Harry kept in contact throughout his life.

"We survived a few skirmishes together and were great friends. He was a terrific fellow."

It was Christmas 1943, and Harry and the other New Zealand soldiers returning home were taken to Advance Base for a week before sailing to Maadi on a Polish ship.

"It was dirty, with awful food but we made it all right. One of our gang, Allan, was laid low with pneumonia and put in the New Zealand hospital where we were able to visit him at any time. When we knew we were about to embark on our voyage home, two of us went to the hospital to see if they would let Allan come with us but they refused. He eventually left on another ship, which was sunk in the Indian Ocean. He floated on a raft for 10 days with some others before they were found. Allan kept them all alive by taking over the daily rationing of what little food they had."

At the hospital Harry visited another patient, Ian Van Asch, an officer whose hands were badly injured after his tank had been hit.

"Another friend, Tiny Kerse, typed a letter to Ian's family, which I brought home to give to his mother. Tiny tried to imitate Ian's signature, but when I gave the letter to Ian's mother later, she was too wise. She said, 'That is not Ian's handwriting. Don't lie to me. Do you think he'll ever use his hands again?"

Ian Van Asch made a good recovery, and after the war, ran Muller Station in Marlborough.

Harry eventually embarked on the trip home on a refrigeration ship, which was heading out to Australia to collect meat. The

Governor of New Caledonia, his wife and two children, and some Australian war wives were also on the journey.

"We had a happy trip, and spent time helping the cooks, running the entertainment, and otherwise playing jokes on one another."

The ship arrived at Port Lincoln in South Australia without incident, and Harry and the other returning soldiers enjoyed 'first class hospitality' with the locals, who put on mutton dinners and puddings, the sort of food the men hadn't eaten for years. After unloading salt from on board the ship, they sailed for Sydney. There, they left the good ship and its Captain, 'a fine man who had retired but came back for war service', and boarded the old *Wahine* for the trip to New Zealand. The ship, launched in 1913 had served as a minelayer in World War I, an inter-island ferry running between Lyttelton and Wellington, then as a troopship in World War II. It is not to be confused with the Union Steam Ship Company of New Zealand's other ship named *Wahine*, which sank in Wellington Harbour on 10 April 1968 while operating as an inter-island ferry on the same route, with the loss of 53 lives.

As the ship left Sydney and set sail across a mighty rough Tasman Sea, Harry was finally on the last leg of his journey home. The *Wahine* sailed into Wellington, and the next day, Harry crossed Cook Strait to return to his mother's home in Blenheim, at the top of the South Island.

A reception gathering had been organised for Harry that evening. But following his long journey and with his excitement to see his mother, who had been on her own since his father died in 1941, the reception was an event he would rather have skipped.

"People who never had any intention of going to war made some fine speeches of welcome, but I just wanted to be home with a few of my family and friends. It was very hard for me to be away when Pa died and to come back to my mother on her own."

As he settled back into civilian life at his mother's home, the true effects of the war on Harry's nerves became apparent, and he realised he was shell-shocked.

"My nerves were completely shot after years spent living on the edge, and under constant enemy attack. The Air Force was flying Harvards over Blenheim at night and I couldn't stand the noise. I knew I had to get out and be somewhere quieter."

The army gave Harry three months leave, a free rail pass and vouchers for thirty gallons of petrol, so he, Bert Murdock and Dan O'Sullivan took off for Wellington where they spent an enjoyable few weeks 'doing nothing' apart from travelling around and having fun.

"If anyone suggested work we left their town pretty quick."

During this time, Harry also had emotional reunions with the wives and parents of several of his late friends who he had served with overseas, discovering how much they were truly missed.

After his break, a refreshed Harry returned to his mother's place at Blenheim, but with the Harvards still flying overhead, he knew he would have to leave for the sake of his rehabilitation. Soon after, he took up an opportunity to move to Hastings, in the North Island, to work as a cabinetmaker at Duncan's Furniture Factory.

"I had never been to Hastings, and was pleased to be able catch up with some of my army friends there, including Len Trew, whose army number was one behind mine. His family adopted me for a while and treated me like a son."

Later, Harry took up private board with the Osborne family in Hastings who 'absolutely ruined' him. He didn't enjoy his job at the furniture factory, largely because the boss 'wasn't a very nice bloke'. After serving out his contract, Harry bought into an engineering firm and was a partner for three years.

"I was the only one with any business acumen. One of my partners was a damn good engineer but a bit unreliable. If he met up with somebody in the afternoon, he mightn't come near the shop until night time."

After the war, in 1946, General Bernard Freyberg became Governor General of New Zealand, and some time later, Harry was excited to learn 'Tiny' was making a visit to Hastings. Harry and some friends from the Div Cav tried to visit the General at his hotel, but were turned away by police. Harry said if the General had known the men were there, he would have surely met with them.

Settling back into civilian life also opened the door to romance. Harry was at a dance when he met a young local woman named Madge, who would become his much-loved wife.

"Madge's mother and stepfather had a cow farm and she used to do the mail run in her little Austin car. She was nine years younger than me. We got married in 1947 and had a great marriage."

A while later, Harry discovered he had inadvertently met Madge's birth father during the war.

"Her birth father was the officer-in-charge on the troop ship which took us to Italy. Unfortunately he wasn't a nice man, to the extent that one of the other chaps and I almost thought about throwing him over the side. He wasn't married to Madge's mother for very long. Although he was an accountant and had a brilliant mind, he was also a playboy. By the time he died at the age of 93, he'd had four marriages and several children."

Harry got on very well with Madge's stepfather Ray, and took up his offer to work on the farm.

Harry and his sweetheart, Madge.

"It was a hard farm with a lot of drains. At one stage, Madge and I ran the 800 acres on our own when her mother and Ray went overseas for eight months."

Harry and Madge later ran Spencer's Grocery Store at Green Meadows near Hastings, before buying their own farm at nearby Maraekakaho, where they were very happy. Sadly Madge couldn't have a family and Harry says adopting didn't appeal to them. However they didn't let this setback hold them back, and gave their time and hospitality freely to countless other children, becoming surrogate parents to many.

"We always had the children of family and friends staying with us. In fact there were people who after they grew up, told us they classed us as their mum and dad," said Harry, who became fondly known to numerous people all around the world as 'Uncle Harry'.

Harry was President of the Divisional Cavalry Association for many years, and was a mainstay of the Hastings RSA, where he was particularly active in the Heritage section, which looked after the welfare of families of soldiers who were killed in the war.

Harry and Madge travelled the world together.

"Quite a few of us acted more or less as fathers to some of these children to keep them on the straight and narrow until they were 17."

He was still involved with the Heritage section in his mid-nineties, although there were 'no customers' then.

Harry was also the founding patron of the website historical project nzdivcav.org, which honours the 2nd New Zealand Divisional Cavalry, and the lives and stories of all who served.

The Spencers had an adventurous spirit and loved to travel, visiting many countries including several Harry had fought in during the war.

"We travelled all over the world, saw many great things and met some very interesting people. We even went to Germany where we were treated like royalty. It was wonderful."

Harry and Madge had a very happy and full life together, which included a lot of charitable and voluntary work for many different organisations.

Harry was still delivering meals on wheels when he was much older than many of the recipients.

Madge Spencer passed away when she was in her late seventies. Harry missed her right until the end of his life.

When he was in his eighties, Harry learned how to use a computer and started to document some of his many colourful and harrowing wartime experiences.

Around this time he also became an enthusiastic user of email, corresponding with people from all around the world. His other interests included golf.

He played for over 50 years and was still playing off a 40 handicap into his early nineties, getting around the course on a Suzuki step-through motorbike, with a special attachment for his clubs. By this stage he had lost his road licence but was able to keep his motorbike at the golf course to use for his golfing adventures.

Harry lived independently in a villa at Masonic Village in Hastings, until he was well into his nineties, where he had all the mod cons including Sky TV and a computer.

Harry was a keen golfer until well into his nineties.

He had friends of all ages, and enjoyed an active social life, with neighbours at the village popping over for 'lolly nights' or to watch All Blacks rugby matches. Harry also loved scones and for a long time made a daily batch, which he despatched to some of his neighbours at the village. Regular visitors also partook in '5pm medicine time' when Harry had his daily tipple of whisky. For most of his life it was his only medicine, he said.

"I don't take any pills. I know a lot of doctors and tell them all they learned at Medical School was how to dish out pills and bills."

Before he enlisted, Harry had helped to build the main trunk railway line between Christchurch and Picton, but didn't take the rail trip himself until 2010, at the age of 94, when a friend took him to the South Island so he could experience it.

Harry continued to honour all the young men and women who didn't make it back from the war. In his later years, he attended a number of commemoration services overseas, including the Battle of Crete Veterans Pilgrimage to Greece and Crete in 2006 to mark the

65th anniversary of the battle, and the Anzac commemorations in Sydney in 2010. In September 2012, Harry, then aged 96, was the eldest of 23 New Zealand veterans selected to attend commemorations in Egypt to mark the 70th anniversary of the Battle of El Alamein.

"It was a great trip. I had several very good friends buried there and it was wonderful to see their graves.

This was Harry's last major trip overseas, as soon after, a stroke impacted his eyesight. By 2013, he was no longer able to email his many friends. In 2014, he moved from the Masonic Village to a rest home in Napier. His body may have slowed a little but his mind and sense of humour remained as sharp as ever. And he still enjoyed his early evening tipple of whisky. In the twilight of his life, as he reflected on his experiences during the war, Harry continued to say war was a 'hell of a thing'.

"I lost some very good friends who were killed, and I sometimes think, what the heck for? What I've learned throughout my life is that the world has a great love for money and this causes most of its problems. War is a waste of good lives on every side."

Harry endured many horrors during the war and regularly witnessed how lives could be lost or saved by a mere whisker. When surrounded by so much death and destruction, and engaging in some of the war's fiercest battles, he couldn't believe how he managed to get through it all with just one minor wound.

Harry enjoyed the camaraderie and friendships he made with many other fine men from right across the ranks, who had also bravely put themselves forward to defend their country and its freedom. He never forgot the good mates he lost during battle, and the others who made it home and passed away after the war. His emotions would rise to the surface when he reflected on the brave young men he had stood alongside, and had shared so much with, but who never had the chance to live the full rich lives they deserved.

Harry's one regret was that he didn't write a book about his life.

"I didn't do it when I was younger because a lot of things

happened that I'm sorry about now. It takes a long time to settle back down when you come home from war. You don't want to talk about it," he said.

On 25 February 2015, this brave, humble 98 year old soldier passed away, 14 years to the day after his beloved Madge. Over 250 family members and friends attended his funeral in Hastings, where speakers included Lieutenant Colonel Sholto Stephens, Commanding Officer of Queen Alexandra's Mounted Rifles, the Armoured Regiment of the New Zealand Army, today's successor to the 2nd New Zealand Divisional Cavalry. A photo tribute, which featured many images from Harry's wartime service, was played at his funeral to the music of Vera Lynn.

Harry Verdun Spencer never did write his book. But he did tell his story. And like so many selfless New Zealanders who so valiantly defended their country, he will be remembered with great affection and respect.

Harry Spencer. Photograph courtesy of Ian Latham.

6

RONNIE

THE SLUMS of Newcastle Upon Tyne in the United Kingdom were a tough place to grow up at the best of times, let alone when Europe was in the grip of war.

With many of the men away in the armed forces, and the women manpowered into essential jobs, or struggling to provide for their families while their husbands were away, it was little wonder many of the poorer children ran wild during World War II.

Among the wildest were Ronnie Sabin, his older brother Eddie and younger brother Joey, who lived in one of Newcastle's most notorious slum areas in a government tenement block known as the Rochester Dwellings.

The two eldest boys had moved into their grandmother's house in the dwellings with their mother, Violet, at the start of the war, when their father, Edward Sabin, a Regimental Sergeant in the British

Army, went off to fight. Soon after, Violet discovered she was pregnant with her third child, Joey. She was just 20 years old.

At the time, Ronnie was only a few months old. He had been born in Dunbar, Scotland, but shortly after, the family moved to a large military training base at Tidworth on the Salisbury Plains. When Edward was called up to fight, Violet had little choice but to move in with her mother. Her relationship with Edward was already falling apart, and she soon found herself the mother of three little boys in wartime, with a husband she rarely saw.

Life was hard for Violet and the boys in the dwellings. The government had built dozens of these apartments to house the nation's poor.

The rent might have been cheap, but most of the dwellings were cold and damp, and many never saw the sun.

Ronnie said the Rochester Dwellings were blighted by break-ins and vandalism, and it was known as the worst estate in Newcastle.

"Our home was on the ground floor in a three-tiered block of twenty-four dwellings, with a large courtyard in the centre. We had a coal range for cooking and an open fire in one room, but we couldn't get warm no matter how hard we tried. We were filthy most of the time, and when we did wear our shoes we had to block the holes in them with cardboard, which we used to rip off the top of Shredded Wheat packets."

Newcastle was Violet's home city. She was born there in August 1919, but spent most of her childhood in Canada where her father took up a forestry job in the 1920s. When Violet was almost 14 years old, they returned to the United Kingdom and settled in Forest Hall on the outskirts of Newcastle. Violet went to school, but left after a few months to become a tailorette in Jackson. Soon after she met and married Edward Sabin.

When she was 91 years old, in 2010, Violet described how difficult it was as a struggling young woman during the war.

"I was only seventeen when I got married. I thought I knew everything but I knew nothing. They were vicious times during the war. You had to grow up quick and it was hard on the women. But we were lucky we didn't have as many air raids or bombs in Newcastle like they did in London."

Newcastle was mainly a target for the Nazi German Luftwaffe in the early part of the war, when a series of bombing raids were carried out between July 1940 and December 1941 on the city's busy docks and railways. Almost 400 people were killed in the bombings, known as the Newcastle Blitz. The last major raid on Newcastle was on 29 December 1941. Smaller scale attacks continued on the city for the next couple of years.

With an absent husband and no welfare, Violet worked hard to support her family. She got a job as a bus conductress and although she worked twelve-hour shifts, six days a week, Ronnie said there wasn't a lot of money left over to feed and clothe the boys.

Violet Sabin with eldest son, Eddie.

"We didn't see a lot of her as she worked long hours and also had a fairly active social life. I imagine the stress of trying to cope with a demanding job and bringing up three difficult boys during wartime would have been more than a lot of women could stand."

The few rations Violet was able to provide had to be split between them all.

"Our diet consisted largely of bread and dripping. We were allowed two slices of bread each. I remember eating my first piece of bread one night and reaching for a second from the middle of the table when my mother got angry because she thought I had already eaten my share. She brought the bread knife straight down on the back of my hand, with the serrated edges making cuts all the way across my knuckles. Blood poured out of the wounds and I tried desperately to suck it all up," said Ronnie.

He only recalled meeting his father once, in 1943 when he was just four years old.

"There was a loud knock on the door one evening and I answered it to see a soldier standing there. I ran down the passage yelling, 'Mummy, mummy, there's a soldier at the door'. By this time our father was a Sergeant Major and was home for ten days leave. Eddie, Joey and I were very excited and loved having him there to play with us and take us to the shops. He treated us to Whitley Bay and Black-rock candy out of his kitbag. Then one morning, just a few days later, we woke to find he had gone without saying goodbye. We never saw him again."

Shortly after, Violet told the boys their father had been killed in the war. They had no reason to believe otherwise until 2001.

Violet intimated the marriage with Edward Sabin was violent.

"The marriage didn't work out. When he came home on leave from the war I knew that was the finish. I wasn't going to be a punching bag for anybody. He was a gentleman outside the house and everyone used to say what a marvellous man he was but he was different when he was on the drink. I wouldn't entertain him after that."

With no father figure in their lives, and little supervision, the boys were out of control from a young age. Ronnie was only four or five years old when he became part of a street gang with other local children, whose wartime childhoods were equally as tough.

"It was an unwritten law in our neighbourhood that the eldest in the family would look after the next one down, and so on. Eddie was very protective of me, as I was of Joey. We formed our own gang, which was assimilated into a larger gang of neighbourhood boys. There were around 14 of us in all, ranging in age from four to 16. Our headquarters was an unused air-raid shelter. New recruits had to be initiated, which mainly involved door knocking or terrorising neighbours. We were cheeky to the extreme and had no respect for older people."

Ronnie said one way to become a fully-fledged member of the gang was to survive a game called 'Kick, Bonny Horse, Kick'.

"The child was blindfolded, taken to the front door of a house and spun around several times. Then they would have to kick the hell out of the door, take off the blindfold and escape before being caught by the irate householder or a member of one of our rival gangs. Some made it. Some didn't."

There were no laws regarding the thrashing of children in those days, so the consequences for the children were often drastic. The police were never called as it was regarded as too dangerous, even for them, to enter the dwellings, said Ronnie.

"They knew if they ventured in they'd get done over for sure, with the older gang members stealing their trousers, shoes, bags, jewellery, watches or whatever they could lay their hands on."

It wasn't long before Ronnie and his brothers also became expert thieves. Anything that wasn't bolted, nailed or screwed down was fair game as far as they were concerned.

The boys' father, Edward Sabin

"We would even steal babies' prams as long as there was no baby inside, just to obtain the wheels for making billy-carts or four-wheeled trollies. The remains of the prams would be thrown in the courtyards of our dwellings along with all sorts of other rubbish. Over time these areas became large-scale dumps, which were overrun with cats, rats and other vermin."

The Sabin's block of houses was the most distant from the shops, so when Violet sent the boys for food they sometimes had to run the gauntlet of the other gangs.

"We usually made it to the shops without incident, but would become frustrated at having to queue for our few rationed wartime items. To beat the boredom we would take turns lining up, which sometimes caused arguments or more serious altercations with others in the queue. On the way home, members from another gang would sometimes try to steal our food. It was rare but if they got away with it our gang was always keen to exact retribution."

The notorious Rochester Dwellings, taken in the early 1970s, but relatively unchanged since the war years when the Sabins lived there. *Photograph from the collections of the Newcastle Libraries.*

With food scarce due the war and the family's economic situation, the boys would often steal food to supplement their meager diet, loading their homemade trollies with turnips pinched from nearby fields, fruit stolen from local orchards, and whatever they could get away with from the local shops.

Orchard raids were a popular pastime for the Sabin brothers and their gang. Ronnie said many of the orchards had brick walls surrounding them and some even had broken bottles cemented to the top, yet nothing could deter the determined young orchard raiders.

"We usually managed to devise a way over, using boxes for ladders and placing wood and sacks on top of the walls. The consequences of getting caught never entered our minds until one dusk raid went horribly wrong. We had navigated the wire fence protecting the orchard and were preparing for a quick getaway with our fully laden trollies. I was up a tree getting the last of the fruit when I saw the owner of the orchard creeping quietly towards the other boys in the fading light. He was carrying a shotgun, which as Eddie would soon discover was loaded with saltpetre cartridges. The pellets were generally used for scaring birds but also proved extremely effective in scaring young boys. From my vantage point I could see the orchardist fire a full charge into Eddie's backside. He yelled in pain and took off for home. I was terrified and didn't want to cop a charge as well so I sat as still and quietly in the tree as I could, and managed to remain hidden until the orchardist finally left. When it was properly dark I hopped down and slipped home. We lost our trollies that night, which meant another pram had to be nicked. Eddie had a sore backside for weeks and reckoned it felt so hot he could have sat in a bucket of cold water and brought it to the boil."

Although food was the main prize, the boys were fairly indiscriminate when it came to their thieving. Ronnie said they would sometimes use their trollies to transport coal nicked from the local rail yard at Tyneside.

"We used to fill our bath with the stolen coal, because if we had left it outside, someone else would have come along and pinched it. We were one of the few families in the dwellings to have our own bathroom, but I can't remember ever using it to get clean."

Boys in the other gangs teased Ronnie mercilessly about his glasses, which he had worn since being hospitalised with a severe bout of whooping cough at the age of three.

The severity of the illness had caused his right eye to turn in and he was prescribed glasses with a black patch covering the left lens to try and encourage his right eye to correct itself.

"I was called 'Lord Nelson', 'Four Eyes', 'Cross Eyes' and many other unprintable names. Those glasses got me into more fights than I can remember. After they had been broken two or three times I decided to get rid of them all together. It wasn't long before my eye came right by itself."

The only occasion when the Sabin brothers' gang fraternised with other gangs was on Guy Fawkes Night.

This was usually celebrated with a big bonfire in the middle of the town square. During the week leading up to the celebrations the children would make up dummy guys or dress up as a guy themselves with a blackened face, harassing shop owners for a 'penny for the guy'. Any money they managed to con would be spent on fireworks.

A couple of serious Guy Fawkes incidents always stuck in Ronnie's mind.

"A small boy was severely burned when someone dropped a lighted cracker into his overcoat pocket, which was filled with fireworks. He started to run off in fright but was pulled to the ground by a couple of adults. They managed to wrestle the coat off him but not before he had suffered horrendous burns to his arms and legs."

Worse was to come. A boy who was dressed as a guy, complete with padding, overcoat, and a facemask, was being paraded around the local shopping centre.

"He was taken to the butchery where the butcher mistakenly thought he was a dummy guy. 'That's a fine, plump guy,' he said, and stuck his knife straight into the poor boy, severing his intestines. He died as a result of his injuries. I'm not sure whether the butcher faced any charges as a result of this tragic accident but it is something I will never forget."

Although they were barely school age, the Sabin brothers had to learn how to fight with their fists in order to survive their bleak life in wartime Newcastle.

"It was rare that any weapons were used in all the rumbles we had with other gangs. That said we had no compunction throwing stones through windows. Some members of our gang also became extremely proficient with a slingshot. This was made out of two pieces of string attached to a small pouch filled with stones, which would be twirled above the head before one end of the string was let go. The results were often devastating. We also used rubber catapults loaded with spent bullets we had picked up at the local rifle range, where the Home Guard practised their shooting skills."

Ronnie said he and his brothers also did their bit for the nightly wartime blackouts by firing stones or bullets at porcelain insulating cups on power lines.

"When these were smashed you could guarantee the power would go off over a large area. We thought this was great fun and enjoyed creating as much havoc as possible. The Germans really had no need to bomb Newcastle. We were doing a pretty good job of demolishing the city ourselves."

School held no interest for the rebellious Sabin brothers, however the local authorities insisted they be enrolled. The boys played truant from the first day along with many other boys from the housing estates in the area.

"Although still so young, my brothers and I were feral and developing into the worst possible type of kids. We were destructive, dishonest no-hopers who were already on the fast track to a life of crime. It was the survival of the fittest in the slums during the war, and we needed to have that fighting instinct to survive."

Despite her children running wild and ending up in constant trouble, Violet had a rosier view of their childhood.

"It was a very hard life, believe you me. But I had a good job and good wages. The boys were well fed and well dressed. They went to school every day. I used to have to walk quite a long way to start work. I would leave the house at 2.30am to pick up the bus at 4am. I would finish work and be home at 2pm, in time for the boys coming home from school. Then they would go out to play. I never knew where they were mind. In the holidays Ronnie and Joey used to go to the seaside area and I'd give them some money. Eddie liked to play football with his mates. My mother looked after them a lot of the time. She was in her sixties then and in good health. I'd say she spoiled them more than anything else."

Life didn't get any easier for Violet and the boys at the end of the war. She worked hard to keep the family afloat but it was difficult as a single woman with no husband or welfare to support her. Her social life continued to take up much of her free time, which meant she was rarely there to watch over or guide her children towards a better path.

The war years were tough on the family and although their living conditions improved a couple of years after the end of the war, the boys' behaviour didn't.

In 1947, Violet, her mother and the boys moved into a new house in Goathland Avenue, Benton. This was a vast improvement on the Rochester Dwellings but there was still no extra money for food or heating, said Ronnie.

"With empty bellies and even less supervision than before, our wild, destructive behaviour continued to spiral out of control. As we grew older stealing wasn't enough to keep us amused and we became hell-bent on vandalism as well. The local council tried to build a block of pre-fab houses in our street in which to accommodate the poor, and we thought it was great sport to try and demolish them as quickly as they were being built. We trashed them, breaking all the windows, smashing the toilet pans and ripping off the doors and cupboards. We simply had no respect for people or their property and were known as the most destructive kids in the district. By this time we had also built quite a reputation with the local police who questioned us regularly about all manner of misdemeanors. Eddie was developing a glib tongue, and as the eldest was our spokesman although we were all adept little liars."

Eventually, in 1950, after years of dealing with the young tearaways, the police and local authorities had had enough. The worst children, including the three Sabin boys, were rounded up and declared Wards of the Court. Soon after the brothers learned they were being sent to Fairbridge Farm School in Molong, New South Wales, Australia under the Child Migrant Scheme.

The exact details of how this occurred remain unclear.

"It is probable the powers-that-be decided it would be good for the whole of the country if my brothers and I were transported to the colonies. The Fairbridge Organisation must have discussed the possibility of us being assessed as child migrants with our mother. However it is difficult to get a clear picture of what happened as our mother told several different versions of events over the years."

The Fairbridge Child Migrant Scheme was well established by this time. It was founded by Kingsley Ogilvie Fairbridge, a Rhodesian philanthropist and Rhodes Scholar, who during a visit to England in 1903, was shocked to see impoverished and malnourished children growing up in appalling conditions in London slums with little hope or prospect. He thought about the wide, open spaces of Rhodesia and wondered if there was a way poor children from London could be sent to South Africa where they could be trained as farmers.

A decade later the first Fairbridge Farm School opened, not in Rhodesia, but at Pinjarra, near Perth in Western Australia. The Fairbridge Organisation later established a second Australian farm school at Molong, and additional institutions in Rhodesia and Canada.

Many other organisations and institutions also ran child migrant schemes during the 20th century, with the motivation of most being to assist seriously deprived children such as the Sabins to seek a new life in a new country away from their unfortunate surroundings and grim backgrounds.

Violet's story of how the boys came to be sent away to Fairbridge Farm School in Australia changed several times over the years, and she never took responsibility for signing the papers which allowed them to go. Despite telling the brothers their father had been killed in the war, Violet later told family members that Edward Sabin had turned up out of the blue when she was at work and had convinced her mother to sign the papers.

In 2010, she said:

"I think he brainwashed me Mam. He turned up with lots of photographs of Australia and told her he was going to train racehorses and that the boys were going to be with him. He convinced her they would be better off with him. He was a Sergeant Major and a good talker. I think he talked her over. Me older sister, Betty, agreed with me Mam as well and thought it would be better for the boys. They

Kingsley Fairbridge

didn't know the life I had before and there was no way I wanted them to have that life again. There was a bit of a dispute between me and me Mam. I wasn't there when she signed the papers in my name because I was at work. I tried to go to court to keep the boys in England but lost the case and the boys were sent anyway. As far as I knew their father had gone to Australia too."

Ronnie said it was an unlikely explanation, as his only recollection of his father was the one visit he made home in 1943. After that he had made no effort to contact the boys again.

"Whatever the case, we were duly assessed by the Fairbridge Organisation which consisted of a medical examination and an IQ test. The medical comprised a urine test for which we were all asked to pee in a bottle. Eddie and Joey had some difficulty with this, but I had no problem at all, so I poured a bit of mine into each of their bottles and we were all declared healthy."

For the IQ test the boys were shown a picture of a bicycle with the front wheel missing alongside a separate drawing of a wheel.

"We had to tell the assessors what was needed to complete the drawing of the bicycle and the budding Einsteins we were, the three of us passed the test. With a clean bill of health and being boys of undoubted intelligence, the Fairbridge Organisation was willing to take us on."

The Sabin boys were booked to sail to Australia on the SS Asturias on 30 August 1950 but had to complete a six-week orientation course at Creagh House in London first.

They packed up the few belongings they could carry, and it was soon time for them to leave their mother, grandmother, and Newcastle behind.

"Our mother came to the railway station to see us off. I remember watching her wave goodbye from the rear upper-deck window of the bus as she left. This was the last image I would have of her for the next 36 years. Joey was only nine years old and he cried bitterly in my arms as we waved goodbye. I had tears in my eyes too, but Eddie shed no tears at all. We were emotional and frightened and wondering what was going to happen to us. Yet despite everything we still loved our mother. As we waited to board the train to London I tried to comfort Joey. Inside, I could feel my heart breaking."

Violet also remembered the day:

"It was heartbreaking when the boys went away. I'll never forget it, ever, ever. I hardly ate or drank for the first six months after they went and I was pretty ill for the first couple of years because of the stress. Fairbridge kept in touch with me. I got one or two letters but then I lost touch with the boys altogether. They went their own ways and I didn't get any letters at all."

The Sabin's Newcastle neighbour Pat, later told Ronnie his grandmother was incredibly upset when the boys were sent away.

"Pat said she often saw her standing out on the street calling for us at dinner time, even though we were long gone. One night she put the chip pan on to cook dinner and nearly burned the house down. She was outside calling for us in vain, forgetting we were on the other side of the world."

Joey, Eddie and Ronnie Sabin in their new
Fairbridge uniforms during their orientation course
in London.

Once they arrived in London, the brothers' six-week orientation course began immediately at Creagh House, a three-storey building not far from Trafalgar Square.

"The aim was for us to get to know some of the other children preparing to sail to Australia. We were also supposed to learn some basic reading skills and receive our first taste of Fairbridge discipline. This would prove an almost futile exercise for the two kindly women in charge, given our backgrounds. Eddie, Joey and I were part of a group of 13 boys who shared a large dormitory. Boisterous pillow fights and wrestling matches took precedence over learning and we created a hell of a mess in the house."

Soon after their arrival, the boys were outfitted in the Fairbridge uniform, comprising khaki shorts, shirts, ties, socks and new shoes. Shoes, while not a novelty were certainly a luxury as the boys had nearly always run barefoot in Newcastle apart from when they were kicking down doors in gang initiation ceremonies.

Creagh House had a large internal stairwell with landings on each floor. The boys thought it was great fun to stand at the top and drop pillows onto people below, particularly if it was the ladies in charge.

"It was relatively harmless fun until one day our boisterousness got the better of us and events took a serious turn. We decided that pillows were too soft so lifted a padded footstool or 'dumpy' onto the top landing. It was my job to score a hit on one of our caregivers as she came up the stairs and it wasn't long before I landed the perfect shot. The dumpy hit her squarely and she tumbled down the stairs. 'I got her, I got her,' I yelled. But my jubilation soon turned to terror when I realised she had collapsed unconscious on the floor. I was sure I had killed her. In my panic I escaped out of the dormitory window onto the roof where I sat huddled in a corner. The police came and the lady was taken to hospital with a suspected broken neck. The incident knocked the living daylights out of me and it was about five hours before the police were able to entice me in. Thankfully the woman hadn't broken her neck but she was badly concussed and never returned to the house again."

After this terrible event the boys came across Frederick Kynnersley Smythies Woods for the first time, a man who would have a significant influence on their lives.

'Woodsy' as he was known had been principal of Fairbridge Farm School at Molong in New South Wales, Australia for several years, but at the time of the incident was in England with his wife on a fundraising mission. At six foot three and nineteen stone, the imposing South African's sheer physicality and strict but fair approach quickly commanded a degree of respect from the young miscreants.

"The Fairbridge Organisation called the couple in immediately to restore order at Creagh House. I was spoken to severely about my actions and was lucky not to be punished. I was nevertheless very frightened and resolved not to get up to any of those tricks again. The episode gave all of us boys a wakeup call, and Woodsy soon had us behaving reasonably well."

Frederick 'Woodsy' Woods and his wife Ruth.

As the boys' departure date for Australia loomed ever closer they developed a new obsession, catching pigeons.

"We set up a trap on the roof and managed to ensnare quite a few. But we'd always let them go. The fun was trying to catch them, not hurt them." Ronnie said Mr and Mrs Woods took the children at Creagh House on many trips around London, visiting the Tower of London and Trafalgar Square where Ronnie was delighted to see pigeons galore.

"Woodsy loved taking us to Hyde Park. He would march us down to the river in our Fairbridge uniforms and line us up to feed the ducks. But feeding ducks wasn't for me. I was hell-bent on getting back to those pigeons at Trafalgar Square and would run off. After a couple of failed escape attempts Woodsy finally lost his patience with me. He had to supervise a large group of boys and couldn't be chasing an itinerant, pigeon-obsessed 11-year-old kid across London. The next time we went to the park he brought two pieces of rope, which he used to tie my hands behind my back and leg rope me to a seat. I asked a few passersby to undo the ropes, but they ignored me. Woodsy kept an eye on me from the riverside but I was going nowhere. It was my first introduction to his unique discipline methods."

The Sabin brothers and other young child migrants at Creagh House, London, being prepared for their new life.

At the end of the course the brothers were considered ready for their six-week journey to Australia. It was a late summer's day when their group of 13 boys together with Mr and Mrs Woods boarded a train from London bound for the southern port of Southampton.

They were sailing on the SS *Asturias* a 22,000 ton vessel, which had made her maiden voyage on the Royal Mail Lines service from Southampton to La Plata, Argentina in 1926. During World War II she had been fitted out as an armed cruiser and was put into service. In 1943 she was torpedoed by an Italian submarine and abandoned in Freetown, Sierra Leone until the British government took her over in 1945 and towed her to Belfast for repairs. From 1946–1952 the *Asturias* served as a migrant ship, making 23 trips to Australia. The majority of the migrants sailed under an assisted passage scheme although there were also fare-paying immigrant families and groups of child migrants.

The Sabins were among around 200 child migrants on board the *Asturias* bound for facilities run by the Fairbridge Organisation and other institutions such as the Methodists, Dr Barnardo's, Catholics, Salvation Army, and Presbyterian Services.

Ronnie remembered arriving at Southampton mid-morning and seeing a huge crowd gathered on the quay alongside the ship.

"Bands played, people were singing, and many were crying. I stood on the wharf and looked up at the *Asturias* in awe. It was massive, like nothing I had ever seen. We grabbed our suitcases and Mr and Mrs Woods ushered us up the gang-plank. Once on board they intro-duced us to Brian and Val, a young couple immigrating to Australia who were our caregivers for the journey. They helped us to find our quarters and we were lucky to be allocated a four-berth inside cabin on a lower deck. We shared it with David, a boy

A young girl setting off for a new life with the Fairbridge Organisation.

the same age as Eddie who was also bound for Fairbridge. We dropped off our suitcases and returned to the deck. As we said our goodbyes to Mr and Mrs Woods we didn't realise we would see them again in three months on their return to Molong, and had no idea of the future impact they would have on our lives."

There was a real party atmosphere on board, with groups of people everywhere, streamers being thrown to people on the quay and balloons and flags flying in the breeze. The ship gave two loud toots and the visitors were ushered back to shore.

"Towards mid-afternoon more toots were heard and then almost before we knew it, the ship began to slip slowly away from the wharf. I stood silently on the deck listening to the crowd singing, *We'll Meet Again*. I wondered whether we would ever see our mother again and if she was in the crowd watching our departure. Joey was crying and I could feel the tears running down my cheeks as I went to find the other boys."

With a free rein to go anywhere on the ship apart from the engine room the brothers immediately set off to explore.

"It was great fun until we hit open sea and things started to get a little rough. I became violently seasick and spent a long time in our cabin being cared for by Brian and Val before feeling well enough to venture back out onto the deck. The only consolation was that I wasn't the only one suffering."

After a few days Ronnie found his sea legs and was soon scheming with the other children about what sort of mischief they could get up to.

"Someone devised a brilliant game called 'Demolition Deck Chairs'. Two boys would stand near the railing towards the stern of the ship and hold a canvas deck chair up in the wind. The trick was to let it go at the right time so it would be carried the furthest out to sea. Some of the bigger boys achieved amazing results but it was dangerous to the extreme, particularly for us smaller boys who were almost carried overboard with the chair. It was great fun, but as they say all good things must come to an end. About 40 chairs disappeared before the crew finally caught onto what we were up to. They left us in no doubt what would happen if they caught us doing it again. The deckchairs were kept under close watch from then on."

The game might have come to an abrupt end but the children were never bored, as they were able to join in all sorts of organised entertainment.

"We played table tennis and deck quoits and the older boys liked to use the gymnasium and weights. There were plenty of sing-alongs, usually with one of the adults on the piano, and a movie was shown every few days, which was a huge novelty for us. Brian and Val looked after us well and made sure we were always tidily dressed. Our shoes were kept polished and we were not allowed into the dining room unless we were properly kitted out in our Fairbridge uniforms."

Meals were taken in two shifts, with the children and their caregivers eating first, followed by the adults. Ronnie said the food was good with meat and vegetables every night.

"We were allowed some flexibility over breakfast. If we were too tired or lazy to appear at the dining room there was no call for us to do so. The caregivers didn't seem to mind. They were probably happy to know their charges were still in their bunks and not getting up to mischief somewhere else on the ship."

As the *Asturias* headed towards the Mediterranean, it hit some more rough seas and Ronnie had another couple of bouts of seasickness. The temperature was becoming progressively warmer and the boys started to have frequent cold showers to combat the heat.

"Our first port of call was Malta, where the ship docked for half a day for refuelling. Brian and Val took us ashore, but we only had the land under our feet for a brief time before we were ushered back on board. If we thought Malta was hot it was nothing compared to our next stop, the northeastern Egyptian city of Port Said. It was stifling and quite a shock to the system given we had only experienced England's murky summers and freezing winters. As we sailed into port we could see soldiers lining the shore, Arabs on camels, and miles of golden sand. Brian and Val were allowed to take us sightseeing and we couldn't wait to get ashore. It was an experience never to be forgotten. We saw camels up close and immersed ourselves in the chaotic, noisy markets, all while trying to cope with the extreme heat."

It was quite an eye opener for three young boys from the wartime English slums.

"We were fascinated by the Egyptian merchants trying to ply their wares to the ship's passengers. Their persistent haggling continued even when we were all on board the *Asturias*. They would sail up in their small craft, a line would be dropped over the side of the ship and the haggling would start, usually over clothing items or silk scarves. The passengers and traders would debate good-naturedly over whether the agreed sum should be lowered to the merchant first, or the goods should be hauled up to the ship before the payment was made. It all seemed to work out in the end."

After the *Asturias* left Port Said, it cruised along the awe-inspiring Suez Canal, where it was dwarfed by many of the large ships it encountered on the 193-kilometre waterway.

The next stop was Aden where it refuelled and took on water.

"Unfortunately the water was not terribly clean and many of us came down with dysentery. The ship's doctor was kept busy tending to us but finally managed to return everyone to good health within a few days."

From Aden, the ship sailed through the Indian Ocean towards Australia, making a couple more stops before it finally berthed in Fremantle.

"The child migrants who were bound for institutions in Western Australia disembarked here for good. We were also told to leave the ship amid some confusion. We were halfway to Pinjarra on a bus when the mistake was realised and we were returned to the ship. It was another three days of sailing before we finally reached Sydney."

Ronnie says the brothers were excited and pleased when the *Asturias* docked for the last time after a long and trying trip.

"I remember thinking of Mum and Newcastle frequently on the journey but we had been so busy while on board that I hadn't really had time to feel homesick. We had travelled halfway around the world and had no idea what to expect. All we knew was that our new life, whatever that meant, was about to begin."

———

There was no time for sightseeing or forming an impression of their new country, as Ted Tepper, the acting principal of Fairbridge Farm School, wasted no time in getting the latest intake of child migrants off the boat and onto the road.

"After quick goodbyes to Brian and Val we were herded into an old Bedford truck for our journey to Molong. The truck was probably an old army vehicle as it had uncomfortable wooden seats along the side and a canopy over the top. With no windows our view was limited to what we could see through the open end at the back."

The boys endured a hellish five-and-a-half-hour journey following the Western Highway over the Blue Mountains through Lithgow, Bathurst and Orange.

Fairbridge was another 30 kilometres past Orange and about seven kilometres before Molong.

"It was a hot day, which got hotter still as we made our way inland. The roads were mainly gravel and the canopy sucked the dust into the back of the truck where we sat. Mr Tepper hardly stopped the entire journey and we were hot, tired, dirty and thirsty by the time we reached Fairbridge Farm School later that evening."

As the truck travelled up the long gravel driveway the boys caught their first glimpse of the 1500-acre property that would be their new home.

"We had never seen so much space, and after the slums of Newcastle it looked like heaven. That impression would quickly be dispelled however, at least for us Sabin boys."

The truck was met by several 'cottage mothers' who told the newly minted child migrants which of the 14 cottages in the Fairbridge village would be their new homes. Ronnie and his brothers quickly learned they would be separated.

"It was devastating as we had never been apart in our entire lives. We had always shared everything and slept in the same room. Later we were told brothers were always separated to prevent them from ganging

The infamous Ted Tepper.

up on other children in the cottages but we were not interested in this logic. We just wanted to be together."

Eddie and Joey were taken away with Joey crying loudly. Ronnie didn't realise he would see his brothers again the next morning and became upset.

"I was dragged, kicking and screaming to Red Cottage where my cottage mother Mrs Blackburn and Mr Tepper tried to reassure me that Eddie and Joey would be fine. By this time I was beside myself and couldn't be consoled. I wrestled away from their grasp and ran off to try and find my brothers. They soon caught me and as I fought to get away again, I shouted every expletive I could think of, which even at the tender age of 11, was quite a few."

Mrs Blackburn suggested a cold bath might be the only solution, so Ronnie was dragged to the bathroom where the bath was three-quarter filled with freezing water.

"I was unceremoniously thrown in, clothes and all. This made me yell and swear even louder so Mr Tepper dunked my head under the water. I came up gasping for air and gave them what-oh again, which earned me more of the same punishment. This carried on until I was finally exhausted and realised the futility of my actions. I was stripped, dried off and dressed in a pair of pyjamas before being taken to my bed in the large dormitory in Red Cottage. I sobbed myself to sleep as I thought of Eddie and Joey and wished we were all back in Newcastle. After all the wonderful stories I had heard about Fairbridge and Australia it was hardly the welcome I had expected."

Despite their rough start, the Sabin boys eventually settled into life at Fairbridge. They were given a stable upbringing under the guidance of Mr and Mrs Woods, who brought up their own four children alongside the hundreds of underprivileged youngsters at the farm school. Ronnie said the cottage mothers did most of the day-to-day caring for the children in the cottages and had the biggest influence on their wellbeing.

"With no qualifications required for the role and little remuneration it was pot luck whether you had a good cottage mother or not. By and large they did a good job but there were some women who had no basic understanding of communication, empathy or how to discipline children in a fair manner. A few were entirely unsuitable and known for their cruelty."

Ronnie said lack of privacy was one of the biggest disadvantages of life at the farm school.

"Our lockers were the only place to store our few personal belongings, and it was impossible to keep hold of a treasured possession."

A strict routine consisting of chores, meals, school, homework, organised recreation, sports, Brownies, Girl Guides and Scouts kept the children at Fairbridge well occupied and mostly out of trouble, although given their backgrounds there was plenty of hijinks.

"We were organised within an inch of our lives but being natural pranksters there was always time for a few tricks."

Fairbridge Farm School, Molong, New South Wales, Australia

The vast expanse of the Australian landscape was quite a shock for the Sabin boys after the English slums, but they quickly took to rural life and enjoyed the bushcraft and survival skills taught by Woodsy on camping expeditions.

"It was a real adventure. We camped in the open and cooked on open fires. We also learned how to fish for yabbies, eels and trout in the river near the farm school. Snakes were a constant danger during the camps and we had to carry a snakebite kit on our belts. I found out later this wouldn't have been effective at all if we'd been bitten by a poisonous brown snake."

Boys at Fairbridge learning bushcraft skills from Woodsy.

With school having played little part in the Sabin brothers' lives in Newcastle, they were relatively unimpressed at having to attend Fairbridge Farm Public School, the onsite primary school run by the Australian government. Older children attended the nearby Molong High School.

"I regarded school as a waste of good playing time. It was a couple of years before I knuckled down but school would never be a high priority. I did enjoy the sporting activities and weekend freedom at

Fairbridge, but deep down the hankering to return to the free and easy life and lack of discipline in Newcastle never left me."

Ronnie said he and his brothers often talked about their mother and going home.

"Fairbridge encouraged us to write letters but Mum was never a good letter writer and I don't remember getting any from her. We were never informed of how our family was or even where they were, although I never asked. I just had these daydreams that the time would come when I would go home. I never imagined for a minute I would be a grandfather before I eventually made it."

What the boys didn't know was that in 1951, the year after they arrived at Fairbridge Farm School, their mother married Andy Rutherford, a personnel officer and paymaster at the dry docks. They didn't have any children of their own, said Violet in 2010.

"Andy couldn't have children. He had a sister the same who adopted two children but Andy didn't want to adopt any. He knew I had my three and he looked all over for them. He used to say 'when we retire we'll go to Australia and find them'."

Ronnie remembered Andy being a background figure in the boys' lives before they left Newcastle and suspects his relationship with Violet was a factor in her decision to send them away as child migrants.

"A simple life with Andy who had a good job on the docks must have seemed attractive to her after the years she had endured bringing us up on her own during wartime and in the tough post war environment."

It doesn't appear Violet and Andy ever attempted to find the boys as she suggested.

The Sabin brothers' desire to return home did lead to one escape attempt, when they and six other boys, all dressed for school, met in a nearby orchard. Once the school bus had returned from dropping the older children at Molong High School, the group set off up the road to the small town.

"As far as we were concerned we were heading for England but how we thought we were going to make it there I'll never know. As we trudged in the heat our shoes became too hot to walk in so we took them off and threw them over a fence. After several miles of walking we arrived in Molong, hot, tired and hungry."

Ronnie's brother Eddie decided the group should try and steal some biscuits and chocolates from the general store, but the store manager was quickly onto them and seemed to take pity on them instead.

"He invited us into the staff smoko room where he gave us a big bag of broken biscuits and some bottles of soft drink. We settled down to our wonderful party without realising the cunning manager was on the phone to Woodsy. Our hearts sank when Woodsy duly arrived, his giant stature filling the doorframe. The party came to an abrupt end and so did our dreams of making it home."

As boys at Fairbridge grew older, they were generally prepared for a career in farm or trade work and the girls for service and house-keeping work. However those who showed an aptitude for their studies at Molong High School and who wanted to pursue an academic career were always encouraged.

Ronnie feeding the hens at Fairbridge.

Otherwise as the children reached the age of around 16, they left their assigned cottages and moved into trainee cottages at Fairbridge where preparation for their future life in the outside world began in earnest.

With school not a priority for Ronnie, he followed Eddie down the trainee path where he was allocated rotating duties in the piggery, dairy, poultry, crops and cultivation, general and machinery maintenance, orchard, and vegetable garden. He also spent time working in the kitchen, bakehouse and laundry.

Girls did domestic training in cooking, baking, kitchen, laundry, mending, sewing and dressmaking.

Ronnie remembered a disastrous junket-making episode when he was on cooking duties in the kitchen.

"I had received full instructions how to make junket and set about preparing 16 large bowls of the loose, milky pudding. Once it was mixed I took the bowls into the chiller room to set. As I placed them on the floor I gave little thought to the nine freshly killed pig carcasses hanging from the ceiling above. That was until I popped back half-an-hour later to check on the junket's progress. Seven of the desserts remained a lovely pristine white. However the other nine had red drops of pigs' blood sitting on the top. In my panic I gave each dessert a quick stir as the junket had not yet set, then moved the bowls to a bench well away from the dangling pigs. The junket was served at lunch and went down a treat. I was asked many times what I had done to flavour and colour the junket, but I never let on. Unsurprisingly I have never made it since."

Mr and Mrs Woods, with their four children, Nyasa, Raymund, Memory and Robert, who grew up at Fairbridge Farm School alongside the child migrants.

Ronnie credited the strict discipline and genuine care metered out by Mr and Mrs Woods for changing the brothers' wild ways and setting them on a more positive path than they may have ventured back in England.

"When I left Fairbridge at the age of 17, Woodsy told me I had been a real challenge and that bringing me up had been like taming a wild horse. We hadn't always been good mates but in the end I shared a warm bond with this giant of a man. He really was the closest thing to a father I ever had."

From the time Woodsy was appointed Acting Principal at Fairbridge Farm School in 1943 to the day he retired in 1966, 1026 boys and girls passed through his care, with each child remaining under his guardianship until their 21st birthday.

When Ronnie left Fairbridge, he followed his older brother Eddie into agriculture, working on a number of farms in Australia and New Zealand as a farm labourer and shearer.

The rough edges may have been smoothed away, but his hard case character remained, and there were many hilarious moments and scrapes in his life post-Fairbridge.

In 1962, Ronnie was working as a brickie's labourer in Sydney when he met Judy James from New Zealand, who became his wife in 1964. By the end of 1967 they were living in Christchurch, New Zealand with their two young daughters, Sonya and Debbie.

The couple started a small butchery in the city, a business that grew into a successful meat processing factory, with over 20 staff and a turnover of more than $2 million a year. Not bad for a boy from the Newcastle slums.

After years of no contact with their mother the boys simply got on with their lives after leaving Fairbridge. Ronnie flourished as a family man and businessman in New Zealand. Eddie enjoyed working in the kitchen of a large hospital in Sydney. Joey stayed in Australia too, working in stores in electrical and air conditioning warehouses and later becoming a foreman.

Ronnie with his future wife Judy James in the early 1960s. They
met in Sydney but later settled in New Zealand.

In 1986, Ronnie received the unexpected news from Joey that
the brother of their old Newcastle neighbour Pat, was visiting from
England and had given him their mother's address.

Incredibly, Violet still lived in the same house in Goathland
Avenue the family had moved into in 1947, while Pat was still living
next door.

The brothers got in touch with Violet and within a few months
she and Andy travelled out to Australia and New Zealand, spending
time with all the boys and their families.

It was a time of mixed emotions for Ronnie, who tried to be
understanding but found it difficult to accept that his mother had
made no effort to contact him over the years.

Although they were reunited, the questions about what had led to
the boys being sent away remained, as Violet was not willing, or able
to share the truth.

This stung even more in 2001, when Ronnie and his brothers
learned their father had not died in the war as Violet had told them,
but had simply deserted the family.

Ronnie's mother Violet, and her husband Andy (back) with Sonya,
Debbie, Judy and Ronnie Sabin during their visit in 1986.

"With the help of the Child Migrant Society we found out that
our father, Edward Sabin, had indeed survived the war, and lived
until the age of 68. His death certificate showed he was a retired
domestic when he died in 1977 following a heart attack. It is unclear
whether he knew what happened to us, but it doesn't appear he ever
attempted to find out. I would certainly have tried to find him had I
known he was alive all those years. It's disappointing we missed the
opportunity to get to know each other."

In 2005, exactly 55 years after he had left Newcastle, Ronnie
finally returned to his childhood home. It was a trip he had dreamed
of all his life.

"It was great to see our old house and to visit all our old haunts
including the site where the Rochester Dwellings once stood. The
most overwhelming part was being reunited with my aunties, uncles
and cousins, and to feel part of my own family for the first time since
I was a boy. I definitely hit the jackpot as they welcomed me back
into the fold and bent over backwards to make my trip memorable."

Ronnie and his mother Violet maintained a civil, but not close relationship throughout her life.

"If she had opened up and been a bit more truthful about the events of the past we may have been able to establish a closer relationship."

Violet died on 9 January 2013.

"I arrived in England on 1 January, so was able to spend a few days visiting Mum before she passed away. She had throat cancer and couldn't speak, but was still able to write a few things down. On the morning she died, I got to the hospital just in time to say a final goodbye."

Ronnie and his mother Violet, during his visit to England in 2005, his first trip back in 55 years.

During the 1980s, many cases of abuse and ill treatment of child migrants under various child migrant organisations started to come to light. By the time Ronnie's book *The Long Way Home* was published in 2010, the schemes were in the midst of international controversy. Apologies were issued to child migrants from both the Australian and

British governments with compensation later paid to many who attended Fairbridge Farm School at Molong. However Ronnie believed without Fairbridge, his life would have been far less successful.

"Although it seems unthinkable a scheme like this could exist today, there were very few options for children like me in the post-war era. My family had been ripped apart by the war and was enduring tough times. There was no welfare to fall back on and we were suffering great hardship. In those days the aim of the Fairbridge scheme was to give children like my brothers and I hope, and the opportunity for a new life. In our case it certainly delivered. I'm convinced we would have ended up in jail or probably tied up with someone like Ronnie Biggs in the Great Train Robbery if we had stayed in Newcastle. Fairbridge saved us and gave us a chance."

A*dapted from The Long Way Home by Jo Bailey with Ronnie Sabin.*

THE END

Thank you for choosing **Never Forget**. If you enjoyed the book, I'd be so grateful if you would consider leaving a **review** on its product page on Amazon as this helps other readers to find it.

Please **read on** for an extract from **The Long Way Home**, the full version of Ronnie Sabin's life story. There are many laugh out loud moments in the book, particularly during his years beyond Fairbridge Farm School. **The Long Way Home** is available as an eBook and paperback from Amazon.

Please visit **jobailey.com** to sign up for my newsletters which are full of writing tips, book news and updates about my writing courses. I'm passionate about coaching people to write their own story or family stories. My **Writing Life Stories Your Way** workshop will be available online during 2022. You can also connect with me at **Jo Bailey Author** on **Facebook**, **YouTube** and **Instagram**.

THE LONG WAY HOME

Available on Amazon by the same author

Published in 2010, **The Long Way Home** is an often hilarious, sometimes gut-wrenching story, which tells the life story of Ronnie Sabin. It covers his early childhood during the war and post-war in the slums of Newcastle upon Tyne, the six years he spent as a child migrant at Fairbridge Farm School in New South Wales, Australia, the 'hard case' years when he worked as a shearer, brickie and labourer in Australia and New Zealand, and the years after he married and settled in Christchurch New Zealand, where he ran his own thriving butchery and meat processing companies.

Ronnie credits his upbringing at Fairbridge and the discipline instilled by its commanding principal, Frederick Woods, for turning his life around and enabling him to make a success of it. However his wild spirit and unique character would never be fully tamed, as some of the riotous stories that feature in the book, will attest.

The Long Way Home adds a positive perspective to the Child Migrant Scheme debate. It pays tribute to the Fairbridge Organisation, and details Ronnie's delight at finally being reunited with his family in England, 55 years after he was sent away.

I hope you enjoy the followed abridged extract:

SHEARING GANG

The shearing contractor I worked for had several large contracts, mainly in the dry, inland areas of Bourke, Nevertire, Nyngan, and Hay. The Australian wool industry was first established in New South Wales, and its origins can be traced right back to the royal merino flocks of the kings of Britain and Spain. The vast, desolate plains of the Bourke district, where we spent much of our time, were known to produce among the best and finest merino wool in the world.

There were around 19 of us in the gang, including shearers, a wool classer, a cook, two pressers and three rousabouts, or 'rousies'.

I initially signed on for a three-month contract in a learners' pen, which was a bit like taking on an apprenticeship. It gave both me, and the contractor, a chance to see whether or not I would make the grade as a shearer.

Before I could start work, I had to join the Australian Workers'

Union, which was a very strong force in those days. It didn't take long for me to figure out who pulled the strings. The union set the pay rates, hours of work, worker numbers and various other conditions. Woe betide anyone who broke the rules.

Most of the shearing sheds were made from galvanised iron and the heat inside was stifling. Tempers would sometimes fray and it wasn't uncommon for the odd shearer to collapse with dehydration. One hot day, one of my colleagues 'Bluey' collapsed on the board next to me and it took four of us to carry him to our quarters. We lay him on the floor under a cold shower until he came to, and gave him a bottle of Guinness stout to drink. He later reckoned it was the Guinness rather than our quick thinking that saved his life. After spending the rest of the afternoon cooling down, Bluey returned to work the next day suffering no further ill effects.

Occasionally a shearer would crack completely under the pressure.

We had to restrain one fellow who went berserk and started to belt a sheep over the head with his hand-piece. It took three of us to subdue him, and we all suffered some kind of minor injury from the flailing piece of equipment.

It wasn't uncommon for us to spend five or six weeks at a time on one of the vast holdings in the Bourke district. One of these properties was the historic merino stud, Uardry, located near Hay, in the Riverina district, which was first established in 1864.

Stud stock from Uardry was sold in Australia and to many overseas countries, including Japan. On one occasion the owner brought several Japanese clients into the shed to watch us work. One of our top blade shearers, a bloke named Jim, immediately dropped his shears, stood back and asked us all to stop work until the Japanese men had left the shed. There was quite a disturbance and the owner insisted that the visitors were his guests and were entitled to watch the proceedings. The situation started to get a bit out of hand, so to try and resolve the standoff, our boss took Jim aside for a private word.

We were amazed, when after their brief discussion, our boss told the owner work would cease entirely until Jim's wishes were met. The owner didn't really have a choice, as had he not agreed, the union would have undoubtedly become involved, with Uardry potentially blacklisted.

The reason for Jim's outburst was soon revealed. He had been a Japanese prisoner-of-war, and said during his imprisonment, he had been hung up by his thumbs with other Australian prisoners to be used for bayonet practice. We were shocked when he dropped his trousers to show us several nasty scars on his legs and buttocks, which were a legacy of his ordeal.

We continued to move from property to property, with new experiences to be had at each stop. One day we were on our lunch break at a property near Cobar, when a young couple and their two children pulled up in an old Holden ute. The fellow got out and asked the boss if there was any work available. He said he and his family hadn't eaten for two days and were all sleeping in the ute. Jobs were hard to come by in those days unless you were sufficiently skilled, and the boss explained he couldn't provide permanent employment. However if the chap agreed to cut a pile of wood for our range, he would ensure the family was fed. I was a bit disturbed the boss would make the man work before giving his starving family any food. It brought back memories of my own childhood when there was never enough to eat.

"Give them a feed first boss," I said. The others immediately backed me up and the family enjoyed their first decent meal in a long time. When we got back to our quarters that night the family was gone, but true to his word, the man had split a decent pile of wood.

When you live and work with a large group in such close quarters there is bound to be a a bit of agro from time to time. One member of our gang, whose temperament left a lot to be desired, was a well-muscled ringer in his mid-thirties known as 'White Slave' who constantly picked on his rousie.

One day, I was working next to White Slave when he was giving his rousie a particularly rough time, swearing at him, banging sheep into him on purpose, then blaming him for not getting out of the way. Another of his mean tricks was to lay the flat side of his shearing comb on the rousie's backside as he bent over. This was not a pleasant sensation and there was always the risk of the rousie being cut. I watched this go on until I couldn't stand the treatment he was dishing out any longer.

"There's no need for that carry on. Give the kid a break," I said. White Slave was livid.

"Keep your mouth shut. If you don't like it, have a go," he replied.

He didn't intimidate me so I shaped right up to him. When the boss and the others saw what was going on, they quickly intervened and managed to break us up before a punch was thrown. Sanity prevailed, if only for a short time, as White Slave was not one to let things lie. He challenged me to fight him outside later in the day, but in the end we agreed to have a civilised punch-up before lunch on the coming Saturday.

Word soon got around about the fight, and wagers started to be laid. White Slave backed himself for quite a tidy sum with several of the gang, and I decided to get a piece of the action myself. I suggested he and I put up £100 each with the winner take all. Given that I was a small bloke and White Slave had a weight advantage over me, he was soon the favourite to win. Nevertheless I was pretty confident I could take him, as I was convinced he was all bluster and didn't have a lot of substance to back it up. As it turned out, I was right. Saturday morning came and I was ready to fight, but it was quickly apparent White Slave wasn't. He pulled out at the last minute, losing his nerve after someone told him I had a bit of experience in the boxing ring. I was very pleased to be £100 richer without trading a blow.

Another real character in the shearing gang was Ray, our Chinese cook. He was a master at his trade who put in long hours to keep our group of big-eating shearers well fed. It wasn't unusual to find him working well into the night, making pies, cakes and other food for the next day. We were appreciative of his efforts. His pies were magnificent and he made beautiful soup. I nearly always had a couple of bowls.

As much as we enjoyed his cooking, our gang was rather unkind to Ray, who was the butt of many practical jokes. We apple-pied his bed (a trick I learned at Fairbridge) and on one occasion put a dead snake in it. He had an old bike, and to annoy him, we would turn the handlebars and seat around, let the tyres down, or loosen the chain.

By the time we put a frilled-neck lizard in Ray's bed he really had had enough. Frilled-neck lizards stand up on their hind legs and hiss when they are annoyed. When Ray hopped into bed and disturbed the lizard he got the full treatment. It gave him a huge fright and he leapt out of bed shouting and screaming.

Not surprisingly, the next day Ray told the boss he had had enough of our stupid pranks and was leaving. This worried the boss, as good cooks were hard to come by and getting another with Ray's ability would be next to impossible. The boss called a meeting and gave us all a dressing down for our stupidity. We were told to apologise to Ray and to treat him better from then on. Ray was then brought into the group and we said our piece, pleading with him not to leave, and promising there would be no more tricks.

Ray was happy. "Velly good," he said. "No more tricks, I no more pissee in the soup."

I had noticed the flavour of the soup was different, but put it down to Ray being a little more heavy-handed with the salt. It never crossed my mind that in his own quiet, and slightly disturbing way, Ray had been getting his own back on us. He certainly had the last laugh. Needless to say, the pranks stopped immediately and normal food service resumed.

ACKNOWLEDGEMENTS

I am incredibly grateful to the special people I have interviewed for this book, Harry Spencer, Bram Uljee, Eva Mulken, Naylor Hillary, Maria Wypych, Józefa Berry, Frania Quirk and Ronnie Sabin.

It has been a privilege to get to know them all, and their trust in me to tell their stories is a responsibility I have taken very seriously. It is not always easy to revisit traumatic wartime events, but these wonderful people told me their stories with such honesty, openness, generosity, and courage. I'm grateful for the permission they gave me to use photographs from their private collections, and written materials including their wartime diaries and memoirs.

The idea for this book came after I had written three stories (about 'Uncle' Harry Spencer, Bram Uljee, and Eva Mulken) for the *RSA Review*, published by Waterford Press, in Christchurch New Zealand. I decided to expand considerably on these three stories for the collection, and add the wartime story of Ronnie Sabin (abridged from my previous book, *The Long Way Home*). I later met Naylor Hillary through one of my business clients, and a fortuitous Facebook request led me to three of the Polish sisters, Maria Wypych, Józefa Berry, and Frania Quirk. The collection was complete.

Thanks to Ian Latham, a passionate historian, and creator of www.nzdivcav.org which honours the 2nd New Zealand Divisional Cavalry, and the lives and stories of all who served. Ian kindly read Harry Spencer's story and provided valuable feedback, which ensured the historical details I had woven into the story, particularly around military terminology and the wartime battles, were as accurate as

Jo Bailey and Harry Spencer, in Christchurch New Zealand, 2010. His story started the journey of *Never Forget.*

possible. Thanks also to Harry's niece, Ngaire Peat for her help with his story.

I am grateful to Jeffery Farrell for supplying images from the Pekanbaru Death Railway for Bram's story. The images were originally from the Argus Collection and feature on Jeffery's website www.pekanbarudeathrailway.com which is the result of many years' work. Thank you also to Bram's wife Jan for her support and help with proof reading.

Thank you to Naylor Hillary's daughter Pam Bissland and her husband, David, for their help with Naylor's story, and Bob Body, a driving force of the Tempsford Veterans and Relatives Association (TVARA) who read Naylor's story and provided valuable feedback to ensure details about 138 Squadron and Tempsford were correct.

Ted Wypych, President of the Polish Association Wellington branch, kindly responded to my random Facebook message, which led me to interviewing his mother, Maria Wypych and her sisters Józefa Berry and Frania Quirk. Thanks to extended members of the family for their help, including Michael Quirk, Di Quirk, Tony Berry, Dorothy and Dennis Gibbs, and special thanks to Bronek Węgrzyn for his meticulous, loving translations of Józefa's wartime diary and Maria's recorded diaries, which were absolutely critical to this story being told.

Thanks also to Ron Sabin's daughter, Debbie Hudson for her ongoing support over the last 12 years .

I'd also like to thank my proofreader, Jo Dickson, who did such a thorough job of fixing up any mistakes and making sure all the finer details were correct, and her late husband John for his valuable feedback.

To my family and friends, thank you for your unwavering support and encouragement throughout the long process of writing this book. It has meant the world. Special thanks to my adult children, Hannah and Riley, to whom this book is dedicated.

Never Forget has been a true labour of love, and I am grateful to each and every one of the people mentioned here for the part they have played in helping me bring it to fruition. If there is anyone I have inadvertently left off this list of acknowledgements, please accept my apology and this message of grateful thanks.

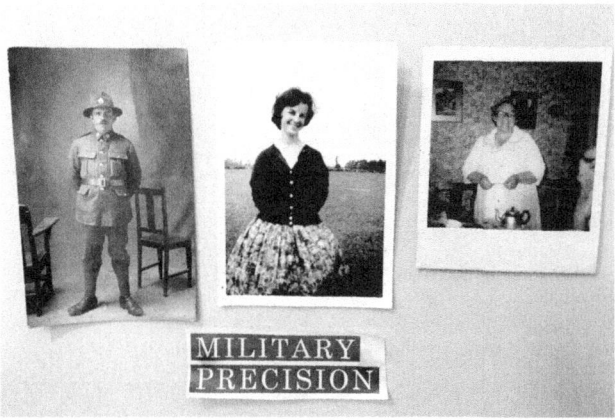

I would also like to honour some of my family members whose photographs were stuck on the wall beside my desk, along with the term 'Military Precision' to buoy me along during the writing process.

They are my great-grandfather Ernie Read (1886–1954) who was in the World War I Reserves (and coincidentally had the same name as one of Harry Spencer's Div Cav friends); my lovely mum, Denise Bailey (1945–2002) who was the kindest, sweetest lady you would ever meet; and my dear Nan, Marion McIlraith (1917–2007), who when she was 90 could still recite poems word for word she had learned in the 1930s. We had so many fun meals and cups of tea around my grandparents' table, which you can just see in this photo. The table ended up with me and my children grew up around it too. It continues to be a daily reminder of the importance of our own histories and the people who have come before.

Jo Bailey

REFERENCES

Personal information sourced from the book's subjects include:

Józefa Berry's wartime diary, written in 1942, translated by Bronek Węgrzyn.

Maria Wypych's audio diary transcribed and translated by Bronek Węgrzyn.

The Wypych family story, by Richard Maggs, 1998.

Harry Spencer's short memoir.

Naylor Hillary's short memoir.

Annie Koetsdyk's letter, supplied courtesy of Naylor Hillary.

The Long Way Home, written and published by Jo Bailey and Ronnie Sabin, 2010

Additional background and historical information for this book was sourced from the following:

New Zealand's First Refugees: Pahiatua's Polish Children, written and published by the Polish Children's Reunion Committee, 2004.

Te Ara – The Encyclopedia of New Zealand www.teara.govt.nz

New Zealand Electronic Text Collection www.nzetc.victoria.ac.nz

New Zealand History www.nzhistory.govt.nz

Ian Latham's website of the 2nd New Zealand Divisional Cavalry www.nzdivcav.org

Jeffery Farrell's website of the Pekanbaru Death Railway www.pekanbarudeathrailway.com

PHOTOGRAPHS

Unless otherwise stated, photographs for this book have been sourced from the subjects of this book:

Bram Uljee, Eva Mulken, Naylor Hillary, Maria Wypych, Józefa Berry, Frania Quirk, Harry Spencer, and Ronnie Sabin.

Pages 11, 16 and 17

Photographs of the Pekanbaru Death Railway and liberated prisoners-of-war. Originally sourced from the Argus Collection and supplied courtesy of Jeffery Farrell.

Page 38

Aerial view of the destruction of Rotterdam, late May 1940. Source: United States National Archives.

Page 47

Infantryman of The West Nova Scotia Regiment in a Universal

Carrier en route to Rotterdam are surrounded by Dutch civilians celebrating the liberation of the Netherlands.

Source: Lieutenant G Barry Gilroy. Canada. Department of National Defence Library and Archives Canada, PA-134390.

Page 91

Soldiers of the New Zealand Divisional Cavalry on a tank at El Alamein, Egypt.

Photograph taken by H Paton part of Paton, Harold Gear, 1919-2010. Ref: DA-02569-F. Alexander Turnbull Library, Wellington, New Zealand.

Page 94

Paton, Harold Gear, 1919-2010. Paton, H fl 1942 (Photographer): Bernard Cyril Freyberg confers with Brigaider Weir at Tripoli during the World War 2 North African campaign.

New Zealand. Department of Internal Affairs. War History Branch: Photographs relating to World War 1914-1918, World War 1939-1945, occupation of Japan, Korean War, and Malayan Emergency.

Ref: DA-02859-F. Alexander Turnbull Library, Wellington, New Zealand.

Page 108

Kaye, George Frederick, 1914-2004.

Badly damaged brickworks near Castlefrentano, Italy, World War II.

Photograph taken by George Kaye. New Zealand. Department of Internal Affairs War History Branch: Photographs relating to World War 1914-1918, World War 1939-1945, occupation of Japan, Korean War, and Malayan Emergency.

Ref: DA-06245-F. Alexander Turnbull Library, Wellington, New Zealand.

Page 117

Photograph of Harry Spencer taken from a video interview with Ian Latham, supplied courtesy of Ian Latham, Georgia, USA.

Page 148

The tent city housing Polish evacuees set up on the outskirts of Tehran. Image: Nick Parrino/Library of Congress.

Page 161

Polish refugee children arriving at Pahiatua Railway Station.

Pascoe, John Dobree, 1908-1972: Photographic albums, prints and negatives. Ref: 1/2-003646-F. Alexander Turnbull Library, Wellington, New Zealand.

Page 210

Naylor Hillary with great-grandson Henry Bissland, cutting the 100th birthday cake at the Centenary celebrations of St Andrew's College, Christchurch, New Zealand in March 2017. Photograph taken by Clinton Lloyd and supplied courtesy of Rector Christine Leighton, of St Andrew's College.

Page 218

The Rochester Dwellings, Newcastle upon Tyne, taken in the early 1970s. Photograph from the collections of the Newcastle Libraries.

Made in the USA
Monee, IL
06 May 2022

96026256R00154